G000019162

SYMBOLS OF LOVE

Stephen Karcher Ph.D writes, translates and lectures on myth, divination, depth psychology and religious experience. An internationally known scholar, he has worked with *I Ching* and other divination systems for over thirty years and has produced definitive translations and commentaries as well as many scholarly articles. As co-director of the *I Ching Project* at the Eranos Foundation, he collaborated with Rudolf Ritsema to translate and produce the Eranos edition of *I Ching: The Classic Oracle of Change*. He is the author of *How to Use the I Ching, The Illustrated Encyclopedia of Divination, Ta Chuan: The Great Treatise* and *The Kuan Yin Oracle: Goddess of Compassion*, the first complete translation of a popular eastern temple oracle. He holds a doctorate in comparative literature and archetypal psychology.

SYMBOLS OF LOVE

I Ching for Lovers, Friends and Relationships

Stephen Karcher

LITTLE, BROWN AND COMPANY

A *Little, Brown* Book

First published in Great Britain in 2002
by Little, Brown and Company

Copyright © Stephen Karcher 2002

The moral right of the author has been asserted.

All rights reserved.
No part of this publication may be reproduced,
stored in a retrieval system, or transmitted, in any form
or by any means, without the prior permission in writing
of the publisher, nor be otherwise circulated in any form
of binding or cover other than that in which it is published
and without a similar condition including this condition
being imposed on the subsequent purchaser.

A CIP catalogue record for this book
is available from the British Library.

ISBN 0 316 85846 3

Typeset in Goudy by M Rules
Printed and bound in Great Britain
by Clays Ltd, St Ives plc

Little, Brown and Company (UK)
Brettenham House
Lancaster Place
London WC2E 7EN

www.littlebrown.co.uk

Contents

Acknowledgements

Symbols of Love is dedicated to Dorte Koch who "speaks the sweet and gracious rhymes of love".

Many thanks for their gifts of friendship and inspiration to Ian Fenton, Enrique Pardo, Jay Livernois, Richard Wainwright, Steve Moore, Rudolf Ritsema, Diana Grace-Jones, Brigitte Heusinger von Waldegge, Luise Scharnick, Esyllt Harker, Charles Boer and James Hillman. Special thanks to Michele Daniel for her reading of the text.

Special thanks to Ken and Elizabeth Mellor, who provided the Reflections and Practices used throughout *Symbols of Love*. Ken and Elizabeth have used *I Ching* for over twenty-five years. As spiritual mentors they have introduced many thousands of people to meditation and other enlightening techniques. Their experience as counselors and psychotherapists and their shared life as a couple makes them particularly at home in the blend of the practical, psychological and spiritual that is the heart of this way of the lover. They founded and lead the Biame Network, an international spiritual community, and teach regularly in many parts of the world.

Foreword

I have worked with the *Classic of Change* for over thirty years. I have translated it, written about it, made it part of my life and, above all, used it to help people on their journeys through life. I am deeply convinced that the spirit of this book and its Way or Tao can guide us and change us, as it has guided and changed people in one way or another for over three thousand years.

In my experience, people come to the oracle with questions in three main areas—love, work and their spiritual path. This book is addressed primarily to those who are finding the Way through love, connection and relationship. It aims to put the considerable powers of the oracle directly at the service of those who love. If you are falling in or out of love, are concerned with what is going on in your intimate relationships or want to know what you can or can't do to influence the course of your relationship, this book is for you.

Our loves and our relationships are intimately bound up with the development of our soul. They offer a sort of alchemy of transformation. We depend on relationships to help us work out our ways through life and to help us see who we are and who we can become. Our relationships preserve us from solitude and isolation and bring parts of us into play we might otherwise never experience. We project parts of ourselves onto our intimate Friends and in doing so come to know ourselves as well as experience the wonder of another being, the amazing epiphany of touching someone truly different. We confront our own shadows and our own needs. We learn about trust and betrayal, love and hate, constancy and change and much more. We explore what it is to be an individual.

The oracle can help us avoid some of the more painful moments and the more obvious mistakes on the Way of love. It can help us see when something is truly significant. It can suggest ways to further and deepen our relationships. It can give us strategies to deal with the intense emotions involved in loving and the problems we face in trying to live our relationships in the outside world.

We invest ourselves deeply in our loving relationships, so deeply that we may need a mirror to help us see what we are doing and advise us of the risks involved. This is what *Symbols of Love* can do. It can warn, encourage, and give you an image to work with. Its basic purpose is to help you find who you really are and what you are really about by suggesting ways you can most successfully interact with your friend, partner or lover. The inter-action, the love, becomes a spiritual journey, full of emotion, passion, enjoyment, friendship and deep connection, making you aware of who you are, what you are capable of becoming and the divine love that surrounds and supports you.

The *Classic of Change* has taught me much about the ways we can, and cannot, love each other. I sincerely hope this tool and this Way can help you on the journey of love you have begun.

Stephen Karcher

Introduction

Welcome to *Symbols of Love*. This version of *I Ching* or the *Classic of Change* has been especially created to help you deal with problems in love and relationships. Using it is not the same thing as reading other books. More than just a book, *Symbols of Love* is an experience, the experience of talking with a wise friend and spiritual guide. It can prompt new thinking, challenge you to change and offer very helpful advice. The more you use the book, the more you are likely to notice that you have entered into a special relationship with *I Ching* itself. The ideas and techniques in this introduction are designed to help you open this relationship, to begin a dialogue with *Change*.

The Oracle of Change

I Ching or the *Classic of Change*, usually simply called *Change*, is a text, a divinatory technique and a spiritual path or Way. It is probably the oldest, most sophisticated and best loved divinatory system in the world. *Change* began in ancient China, about three thousand years ago. First used by shamens, spirit mediums and sages, it became the oracle of the Kings of Chou (1100–500 BCE). They used it to facilitate communication with the spirit world, to order ritual and sacrifice and to suggest political, military and social strategies in critical times. So significant was this practice, that writing evolved primarily in order to record the magic phrases in this book. In the following centuries, the images and practices of *Change* inspired many of the fundamental ideas of eastern philosophy, ideas of the Way or Tao, yin and yang, the qualities of time and the right moment to act, and guidance through contact with the helping spirits or *shen*. The symbols of *Change*, which are presented in this book, gathered and inspired much of what was best in Chinese culture, from medicine and magic to philosophy. The great systems of correlation that characterize this culture, systems that link colors, tastes, sounds, our body and its organs, feelings, historical periods, dreams, directions and even winds and weather in a great cosmic whole, were first evolved through the power of the divinatory symbols of *Change*.

In the middle of the Warring States period (400–220 BCE), a terrible time of war and conflict, several groups of spiritual seekers recognized that this old oracle book was actually a method of spiritual transformation, a Way, and devoted themselves to explaining its use. Their inspiration is at the heart of the book we know now, an integral and magical mixture of practical advice and profound wisdom that can change the way we experience our world and ourselves.

The Way of Change

You will find this Way at the heart of *Symbols of Love*. As an oracle book, *Symbols of Love* can help you understand what is going on in your relationship. Through its symbols, it also opens a path that we can follow. It seeks to connect us and our experience of love with the Way or Tao, the "ongoing process of the real". In the words of a traditional commentary, this enables the people who use the oracle to "follow the order of their nature and of fate."

You begin this process by asking a question and "entertaining" the answer, seeing things in terms of the symbols. The same sort of process applies to your relationships. Over time, the symbols of the oracle focus spirit into the relationship, transforming the way you see your love and desire. It helps free you from compulsive emotions and gives your Friend a chance to be seen in his or her own right. You begin to understand what the spirit of the relationship really is. The oracle's symbols don't just give you information; they transform your imagination until it becomes a kind of sacred space attractive to the spirit.

The Language of Change

There are several words you will find in the oracle book that are fundamental to understanding the Way of change. The first is the most mysterious: *I* or *change* itself. Though it contains the ideas of orderly change, when things are following their natural courses, the word also has more precise meanings. The first is "trouble", a kind of destabilizing change in which what seemed to be solid and secure suddenly shifts and becomes fluid. The second is the response to trouble: creative imagination, emotional mobility, versatility, and the ability to change directions quickly. You are repeatedly advised that in order to deal with trouble, your identity should not be fixed but fluid. It hints that the purpose of trouble is to change the way you think and act so you are more in accord with the Way.

The **Way** or **Tao** is felt to be a great mysterious flow of energy or spirit that animates and shapes the world. It offers a Way or path to each of the myriad beings in the world and gives them their potential identity. To be "in the Way" or "in Tao" is to experience meaning. It brings love, compassion, joy, and creativity. The two basic divinatory signposts used in the *I Ching* show this. The first, **the Way is open**, shows that an action or direction will release creative energy and good fortune. The second, **the Way is closed**, shows that an action or direction will cut you off from the spirit and leave you open to danger.

The Way is thought to unfold through the continual alternation of two primal powers. The oldest words for these two powers are **Great** and **Small**. These later became the more familiar **yin** and **yang**. These are basic ways of orienting your will so as to be most effective in a given situation.

Yang Power or **Being Great** calls on you to collect your strength, focus on a central idea, set yourself in order and act decisively. The Great Person is someone who has done this consistently. Thus, he or she has acquired power and influence, and the strength to help and protect others.

Yin Power or **Being Small** calls on you to let go of your self-importance, be flexible and adapt to whatever crosses you path. Small People adjust to whatever happens in a flexible and spontaneous Way because they are not impeded by an inflated sense of self-worth. It is important to realize that yin and yang or Great and Small do not *mean* woman and man. Women and men are *both* yin and yang, and we all are called on at times to act as Great or Small. The ability to adopt either orientation is of crucial importance in a relationship.

By adjusting yourself to the flow of these powers and the Way behind them, you accumulate a special **power and virtue** called **Te**. This inner strength helps you become who you are really meant to be. It opens you to the power of Heaven and your own deep nature. It can indirectly affect everything around you. It will help your relationship acquire both strength and sincerity.

The ancient sages believed there are many kinds of beings in the world other than humans, but two in particular are of great importance in your search for self-realization and a satisfying relationship. The **spirits** or *shen* and the Eight Helping Spirits are bright spirits that can aid you. They confer power, energy, vitality and confidence and will open doors and clear away obstacles. They ennoble your desires and commitments. The divinatory formula **there is a connection to the spirits** or **you are**

connected to the spirits and they will carry you through refers to these powers. These terms show that they approve of your action and will be there to help you. They can give us many gifts, among them success in an endeavor, effective power and the capacity to bring your situation or relationship to maturity.

Adversity expresses the action of another kind of spirit, the "angry ghost" or *kuei*. This divinatory formula shows that you are facing a danger with its roots in the past: memories, old wounds, unresolved desires or actions. These are usually born in sorrow, pain and anger and act with a great degree of autonomy. They can significantly influence the present. In a relationship, they can come from many directions. Usually the best approach is to face the danger and either exorcise or pacify the bad influence by assimilating it or dissolving its power over you and the expression of your feelings.

The **ancestors** are also a major feature of this landscape, and the word is used often. Ancestral spirits connect us to sources of life. When they are properly recognized and appreciated, they confer blessings (*fu*) on the living. There are important rituals involved in dealing with the ancestors: temple sacrifices, often made by the King for the good of all, shrines and shared meals. There are important sites where these rituals take place: the Ancestral Temple, the Field Altar, the Outskirts Altar, and the Hilltop Shrines or grave mounds. At these sites, contact is made with the ancestors. We can speak with them and partake of their wisdom and blessing. We can all honor these deep wells of tradition and wisdom within us. They are very important parts of the landscape of love.

The Eight Trigrams or Helping Spirits

Another important part of this landscape that you should be familiar with is what is called the Eight Trigrams or three-line diagrams that are thought to represent and invoke the Eight Helping Spirits. Here are the eight trigrams and their associations. They are given in the oldest arrangement called The Order According to King Wen, a cyclic order characterizing the Way these forces work in the world we live in. Take a moment to familiarize yourself with these Spirits, for they are active in all of the 64 Symbols.

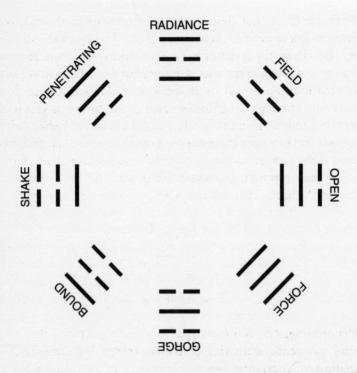

RADIANCE

PENETRATING

FIELD

SHAKE

OPEN

BOUND

GORGE

FORCE

The Order According to King Wen or Later Heaven arrangement

Numinous Spirit is mysteriously active in all things.
Through these figures, change and transformation can occur
and the fates of all things come to their perfection.

Shake, CHEN

Shake, CHEN, is the thunder spirit who bursts forth from the Earth below to arouse, excite and disturb. This spirit stirs things up and brings them out of hiding. It can arouse your dormant energy and give you the strength to undertake difficult things. Its symbol is **thunder** and its action is to **rouse and excite**. It is made of a stirring strong line beneath two dormant supple lines. In the family it is the first son. As a spirit guide, Shake is the arouser and exorcist, driving out the old, rousing and opening the field of the new. He is flamboyant and sexual, luxuriating, frightening and inspiring, green and full of juice. He is motion and moves all things. He is an emerging dragon.

Penetrating, SUN

Penetrating, SUN, is the spirit of wind and wood, a subtle, beautiful and gentle spirit that permeates things, bringing them to maturity. Penetrating can give you the ability to support and nourish things. It is associated with marriage and presides over the new house. Its symbol is **wind and wood**, its action to **enter from below**. It is a supple line that nourishes the two strong lines above it. In the family it is the eldest daughter. As a spirit guide, Penetrating enters and reaches the heart, elegant and powerful, moving like wind and wood in the Earth. She is a healer, matches and couples the beings, lays out the offerings, brings each thing to its fate.

▬▬
▬ ▬
▬▬

Radiance, LI

Radiance, LI, is the spirit of fire, light, warmth and the magical power of awareness, a shape-changing bird with brilliant plumage that comes to rest on things. Radiance clings together with what it illuminates. It can give you the power to see and understand, and to articulate ideas and goals. Its symbols are **brightness and fire**, its action to **hold or cling together**. It is the single supple line in the middle that holds two strong lines together. In the family it is the middle daughter. As a spirit guide Radiance is the bright presence of things. She leads through her warm clear light, through beauty and elegance, the radiance of living beings holding together. She is the bird dancer with brilliant plumes and brings strange encounters and lucky meetings. She is nets and soft things with shells. She is a bright pheasant, bird of omen.

▬▬
▬ ▬
▬ ▬

Field, KUN

Field, KUN, is the womb that gives birth to all things. This spirit nourishes everything, without it nothing could exist and take shape. It can give you the power to shape things, to make thoughts and images visible. Its symbol is **Earth**, its action is to **yield, serve and bring forth**. It is made up of only supple lines. In the family, it is the mother. As a spirit guide Field opens, yields and closes all things into her. She is the flow, the provider, welcome everywhere, the opening that receives the seed of Sky. Her hands give blessings. She receives the dead. She is the mare roaming the Earth tirelessly.

Open, TUI

Open, TUI, is the spirit of open water, the vapors that rise from lakes, ponds and marshes that fertilize and enrich. Friendliest and most joyous of spirits, Open brings stimulating words, profitable exchange, cheerful interaction, freedom from constraint and sexual encounters. It can give you persuasive and inspiring speech, the ability to rouse things to action and create good feeling. Its symbol is the **mists and the lake**, its action to **stimulate**. It is the single supple line that leads two strong lines forward. In the family it is the youngest daughter. As a spirit guide Open leads through joy and cheering words, magic and pleasure. She dances with the *shen* and feels the spirit in her body and gives it words. She is rising mists and open water. She gladdens all things that welcome her. She is a dancing goat and a sheep.

Force, CH'IEN

Force, CH'IEN, is a dragon, a creative spirit that lives in the waters and in the Heavens. It is a dynamic shape-changer and can give you creative power, inspiration and enduring strength. Its symbol is **Heaven**, its action to **persist**. It is made of only strong lines. In the family it is the father. As a spirit guide, Force is tireless creative energy, shape-changing, relentless, riding a dragon, inspiring, creating dynamic harmony. He is dangerous. He is a tiger. He brings deep abiding joy.

Gorge, KAN

Gorge, KAN, is the spirit of rushing water. It takes risks, like water falling, filling the holes in its path and flowing on. It dissolves things, carries them forward and cannot be stopped. It can give you the energy to take risks, to focus your courage at a critical point, to confront and overcome obstacles. Its symbol is **streaming**, water flowing rapidly between two rocky banks, its action to **risk and fall**. It is the single strong line between two supple lines. In the family it is the middle son. As a spirit guide Gorge leads through danger. He dances with ghosts, risks all and always comes through. He exults in work, he dissolves all things. He is a black pig, hidden riches.

Bound, KEN

Bound, KEN, is the mountain spirit, who limits and brings things to a close. This spirit suggests the Palace of the Immortals, the eternal images that end and begin all things. It can give you the power to articulate what you have gone through and make your accomplishments clear. Its symbol is the mountain, its action to still or stop things. It is the single strong line that stops two supple lines beneath. In the family it is the youngest son. As a spirit guide, Bound leads through perceiving and fixing limits. He is nemesis.

He articulates fate. He is the still point in all turning, the refuge of distant mountains. He is a dog, guarding, watching and finding.

Here are the same figures in what is called the Earlier Heaven Arrangement or Order According to Fu Hsi. This arrangement was thought to represent a golden age. It was, and still is, used as a powerful charm against negative influences from demons or ghosts.

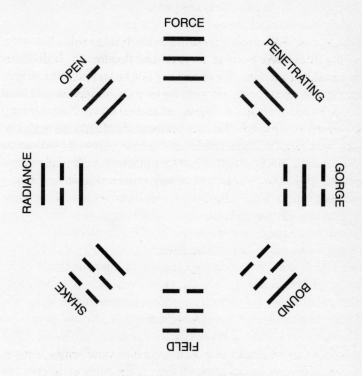

The Order According to Fu Hsi or Pre-Heaven arrangement

On Love and Relationships

Love between two people, sexual, romantic and transforming, as well as the love of deep friendships, is one of the most powerful experiences in our lives. Love opens the mysteries. It can be a gift from Heaven or a forest fire, inspire us or literally drive us mad. Love can be deeply frightening. We don't know what to do; we don't know what may happen. All we are aware of is the desire, the need, the hope, and the emptiness. The oracle can help with this. Of course, it not a love charm; it can't make someone love you. But it can give you information and suggest strategies, ease anxiety and, with luck, help the path of love run smoother.

The character of love changes over time, and relationships give us a Way of evolving with our changing love. Of course, people in different parts of the world have different ideas about love and relationship. We in the west often sentimentalize love or commercialize it. We also have a long tradition of seeing love as a spiritual path, for many wonders are inherent in a loving relationship. Through the love between them, and through the long-term work within a relationship, the people involved can be alchemically transformed. That this possibility, the balance of wonder and work, is inherent in any relationship is a profound spiritual truth.

The idea of a relationship in this book suggests a deep feeling or soul connection between people that has an alchemical, transformative aspect. The need for emotional sincerity is implicit in this sort of connection. It is expressed throughout the book in the word **Friend**. It can indicate a romantic and sexual relationship, an intimate friendship, a working partnership or any other deep relationship that has this alchemical or spiritual potential. Though the oracle of love is not love magic, that is, you can't change someone's heart with it, it can help considerably, because it connects with an old spiritual Way. When you use it, you get both pragmatic advice on how to deal with particular situations and suggestions on what the deeper significance of the problem might be. It can help people in a relationship toward both peace of heart and a deepening of desire.

The Relating Person and the Experience of Paradise

In traditional thought, there is an ideal inquirer or user of the oracle called *chun tz'u* or "child of the chief". This is an old noble title that was transformed into the ideal of the seeker, the one who wishes to live her or his life in accord with the Way, and uses the oracle to help in this quest. Confucius called this ideal inquirer the gentleman or person with nobility achieved through transformation and experience that leads to a clear and open heart and a flexible, loving mind. Through using the oracle and bringing action into accord with the Way, the *chun tz'u* accumulates Te, power and virtue, the power to realize the Way in action and to be who she or he is truly meant to be.

In *Symbols of Love* this figure becomes the Relating Person, one who seeks the Way through love and relation. The oracle is meant to help this person find the experience at the heart of all love, the experience of being "in the Way", connected to the great sources of life and love that nourish everything. This is an experience of paradise, an experience of the love and spirit that permeates everything.

The 64 Symbols of Change, in the second half of this book, describe the landscapes of love in which and through which this quest occurs. They each embody an image that is informing or shaping the lover's situation at a particular time, an inherent image that connects all aspects of the situation, inner and outer, individual and social, physical and spiritual.

These images both unify things and break down barriers. Many overtly center on marriage and union as a metaphor for deep human connection. They involve sacrifice and ritual, relations with the ghosts and spirits, soliciting and receiving blessings from the spirit world, and tactics in difficult situations. Behind all is an experience of the Way and the insight that being in accord with the Way is the most effective way to act in any situation. Specifically, the practice of *Change* was thought to access a bright guiding spirit that would take up residence in the emptied and ordered heart of the one who loves. To use one of the divinatory formulae, this "generates meaningful experience and good fortune by releasing transformative energy."

In this sense, we can understand these symbols as seeds of a sort of paradise that, through assiduous watering and tending, bring divine love into your relationships. They blossom into a direct experience of connection to the Way through the love between two human beings. The pervading images can link thought, feeling and action and release the experience of bliss or union in and through any situation. You can water these seeds of paradise by using the oracle and letting its images shape your imagination.

Reflections and Practices

The reflection and practice suggested with each symbol, provided by Ken and Elizabeth Mellor, is connected with this quest for the experience of paradise. The way they work is based on a particular understanding of our relationships and the parts they play in our spiritual and worldly lives. Both spiritual and worldly dimensions are always present in everything we do. The Reflection and Practice section of each symbol provides simple, practical ways to bring these aspects into balance in your life as you consult the oracle and respond to its answer. They are based on three fundamental truths about relationships.

The first is that human beings are at their true best when they are open, expanded and at one with everyone and everything. This truth, which embodies our connection to the Way, is a fundamental driving force behind everything in our lives, woven into the foundations of our beings. When we close down, contract or separate ourselves, we become congested with unfinished business that we then either hold in or project out. Neither activity contributes to openness or spiritual health.

The second truth is that like attracts like and only what is alike can come together. In practice, this means that everything we perceive about others and what they do is as true of us as it may be of them. If we are together, then we are alike. So all other people's attractive attributes are true of us, just as are their unattractive ones. Many people find this difficult to accept. However, the difficulties are to do with our having contracted or separated ourselves from these attributes and behavior within ourselves in the first place. The challenge is that in opening up again, we face all the discomforts that led us to close down in the first place, not always an easy prospect.

The third truth is that our profound need for openness, expansion and oneness compels us towards freedom, even if we are reluctant. We create situations that stimulate us to release what we hold. Our systems will not tolerate limitation. We do whatever it takes to free ourselves, although at times we may not realize that we are doing so. We give ourselves things to feel happy about and unhappy about. Sometimes we even go to the extent of creating great joys or traumas for ourselves.

Our relationships with others are an ideal ground for this realization. The way this works is simple. Enjoying our Friends is a simple reminder to relish these same qualities in ourselves, neither denying nor projecting them. Similarly, when facing something unpleasant or worse, we are reminded to take notice of and deal with the same things in ourselves. We do this by recognizing them as our own qualities and experiencing whatever goes with them in ourselves. Doing this helps us to release ourselves from our own compulsions and lacks. As we do this, we can generally achieve a deep personal resolution and a much greater sharing and intimacy with all others involved. The oracle can help us realize the importance of relationships in this sense. The advice suggested by the Reflection and Practice sections offers practical ways of promoting these realizations.

HOW TO USE
THE ORACLE

First Step: Finding the Question

One of the great keys to the art of divination and working with the oracle is finding and formulating the right question. Your question focuses the power of the symbols and locates you within the field of images that the book opens for you. Since this is *Change* for lovers and Friends, your question will most probably revolve around concerns such as what is going on in your relationship, your Friend's feelings, the probable course of the relationship, your own part in the relationship or where the relationship could or should be going.

Whatever your concern is, take some time to think about it. Explore your feelings, experiences and memories, desires and anything else that connects to your question. Ask yourself why you are consulting the oracle. Ask yourself what you are afraid of, angry about, grieving for. Above all, find out what you want to know and phrase your question as precisely and clearly as possible.

Ask something important to you and, in general, avoid questions that can simply be answered yes or no. Don't ask, "Does she/he love me?". Rather, ask, "What does he/she feel about me and the possibility of a relationship?". Though you might ask: "Will this relationship work?" and be given an answer, a more interesting way to think about the question might be "*How* can this relationship work out for the best for all concerned?". This gives you the chance of receiving much more helpful advice.

Because this is an oracle for those in loving relationships, you will also find it important to define where you stand as the inquirer, the one who is asking the question. Are you asking as part of an existing relationship? Or are you asking as a seeker, someone who is looking for a relationship? Will the answer apply primarily to you, or to the two of you? The answers you get to these questions will guide you to the question you will ask the oracle. They will also help considerably in understanding the answer, for the oracle's response is directly connected to the question asked.

When you have thought about your question, its associations and its interconnections, and you have defined who you are as an inquirer, you are ready for the actual consultation.

Second Step: Asking the Question

You can use one of several methods to ask your question of *Change*. Each of these methods let you generate the six lines of one of the sixty four diagrams or *gua* that organize and display the book's oracular texts. The lines are counted from the bottom up and form a six-line diagram, a *gua* or hexagram. There are four kinds of lines that may be used to create this diagram:

9 ———○———	8 —— ——	6 ——×——	7 ————
old yang	**young yin**	**old yin**	**young yang**
transforms into >		*transforms into >*	

As you notice, two of these kinds of line *transform* or change shape, each becoming its opposite. When they do, they transform the shape of the diagram, thus creating a second diagram. Here is an example of the potential form of a reading:

```
6 [          ]                          [              ]
5 [          ]   Outer Trigram          [              ]
4 [          ]                          [              ]

3 [          ]                          [              ]
2 [          ]   Inner Trigram          [              ]
1 [          ]                          [              ]
```

Primary Figure   *transforms to:*   **Relating Figure**

Number: _____   Number: _____
Name: _____   Name: _____

Here is an example of an actual completed reading:

Primary Hexagram   *transforms to*   **Relating Hexagram**
Name: *40 Loosening*   Name: *7 Legions*

Generating the Lines

There are several ways to generate these lines, but the best known are the Coin Oracle and the Yarrow Stalk Oracle. I prefer what I call the Token Method. It is direct, elegant and preserves the mathematical ratios of the oldest ways of consultation. All of these methods produce the six lines you need to create a Figure.

The Coin Oracle comes from the Tang Dynasty, and was popularized in the Sung Dynasty, but this type of tossing oracle is found all over the world. You need three coins, each with a head and tail. Old Chinese bronze coins with a square hole are often used. Heads are given the value three, tails the value two.

Throw the three coins simultaneously six times, adding up the numbers each time. Then record the kind of line the numbers represent.

tails + tails + tails = 2 + 2 + 2 = 6 = changing yin line   **6**   ━━×━━

tails + tails + heads = 2 + 2 + 3 = 7 = stable yang line   **7**   ━━━━

tails + heads + heads = 2 + 3 + 3 = 8 = stable yin line   **8**   ━━ ━━

heads + heads + heads = 3 + 3 + 3 = 9 = changing yang line   **9**   ━━○━━

Form your Primary Figure by recording the lines, starting from the bottom up. Then form the Relating Figure by changing the transforming lines. Use the Key to the Hexagrams to determine the numbers and the names.

Existing versions are somewhat unclear in my opinion, so let's try a different one.

The Yarrow Stalk Method is an older, more ceremonial and more complicated form, with a different mathematical ratio between yin and yang. To use it you need a set of fifty thin sticks, about 12–15 inches long, traditionally taken from the tips of the *Achillea millefolium* or yarrow. You divide and count out this bunch of stalks three times to produce one line. Each time you go through this process, you produce a number (six, seven, eight or nine) and thus a line of your Figure.

- Put the bunch of fifty stalks on the table in front of you. Take one stalk and put it aside as the Witness. It will remain unused *throughout the whole process*.
- Divide the remaining bunch into two random piles.
- Take one stalk from the pile on your left. Put it between the fourth and fifth fingers of your left hand.

- Count out the pile on your right into groups of four, laying them out clearly on the table in front of you until you have a remainder of four, three, two or one.
- Put the remaining stalk/stalks between the third and fourth fingers of your left hand.
- Count out the remaining pile in groups of four until you have a remainder of four, three, two or one. Put the remainder between the second and third fingers of your left hand.
- Take all the stalks you have put between your fingers and lay them aside. They are out for this round.
- Make one bunch of the stalks that remain and repeat the entire procedure. Again, put the stalks you have collected between your fingers aside for this round.
- Repeat the process a third time. This time, count the number of groups of four left on the table. It will be either six, seven, eight or nine. This indicates the first or bottom line of your Figure.
- Repeat the entire process five more times to obtain the complete Figure. Enter the lines and make the transformations if there are any. Then use the Key on page 308–309 to find the names and numbers.

The Token Method, which I heartily recommend, combines the ease of the coins, the mathematical odds of the yarrow and an amazing directness, for you do not use the set of four numbers. To use this method, you need a small bowl and sixteen marbles or identically shaped tokens of four different colors: one of a first color; three of a second color; five of a third color; and seven of a fourth color. The one marble of the first color indicates transforming yin; the three marbles of the second color indicate transforming yang; the five marbles of the third color indicate stable yang; the seven marbles of a fourth color indicate stable yin. Put the marbles into the bowl and draw one out. It is your first line. Write the line down, return the marble to the bowl and draw again. This is your second line. Repeat four more times until you have completed the Symbol, then make the transformations. Then look it up in the *Key to the Symbols* on page 308–309.

Using *Symbols of Love*, you can vary or extend this basic method. One interesting way is for each person in the relationship to produce a separate answer, then produce a third figure together, alternating in drawing the tokens to produce it. Here, you can see what each person wants, expects or needs from the relationship and what the relationship itself, the third that is the product of the two, might want or feel. You can also simply make this joint answer by itself by alternating the drawing of the tokens to produce the lines.

Trigrams and their Symbols

The divinatory system of *Symbols of Love* is carried by the 64 six-line diagrams or hexagrams, each of which has a series of different texts attached to it. Because of the transforming lines, each of these hexagrams can change into any of the others. In a reading or answer, as we have seen, there are usually two hexagrams involved. The first, the Primary Figure, talks about the basic situation and how to deal with it. The second, the Relating Figure, shows how you are *related to* the situation. It can indicate a future development, a past attitude that brought you to this point, a warning, a goal, and a deep desire—whatever is relating you to the basic answer.

Each hexagram or six-line diagram is made up of two three-line figures or trigrams, signs of the Eight Helping Spirits we saw earlier. The trigrams were thought to be magical figures that evoked these spirits and connected the inquirer to basic processes in the world around us. In the sort of divination we are doing, the trigrams reveal the relation between the inner and outer worlds and point out the hidden possibility at the core of each Symbol.

When the lower trigram is seen as representing the inner world, and the upper trigram as representing the outer world, we have a dynamic picture of the interaction between what we feel or and what we experience as going on outside us. For example, in *40 Loosening* we find: "Thunder and Rain arousing. Loosening.

Your inner world dissolves and releases rousing new energy in outer activity."

exit	6 [	]	**Outer**
outer centre	5 [	]	**World**
transition	4 [	]	**Trigram**

threshold of manifestation

transition	3 [	]	**Inner**
inner centre	2 [	]	**World**
entrance	1 [	]	**Trigram**

Traditionally, the four central lines of a hexagram are seen as representing two overlapping trigrams. If we unpack them and use them to make another hexagram, we get what is called the Nuclear Symbol or Hidden Possibility. This gives us a sense of a hidden possibility or goal at the center of the situation.

		6 [	]		
		5 [	]	6	**Outer**
Inner	3	4 [	]	5	**Nuclear**
Nuclear	2	3 [	]	4	**Trigram**
Trigram	1	2 [	]		
		1 [	]		

For example, the Hidden Possibility of Symbol *40 Loosening* is Symbol *64 Already Fording*. This suggests that the deliverance or release described in Loosening is a stable process that is already underway.

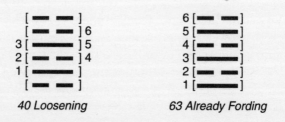

40 Loosening   *63 Already Fording*

Both of these aspects, the Inner–Outer relation and the Hidden Possibility, are described in the texts of each of the Symbols of Love in the section called Symbol, Reflection and Practice.

Third Step: Reading the Answer

You are now ready to read the answer to your question in the *Symbols of Love*. Once you have determined the lines and the diagrams, use the *Key to the Symbols* on page 308–309 to find the names and numbers they represent. Then turn to those Symbols in the book. This material comes from the clearest and most accurate translation now available, a translation made directly from old Chinese. You have the oracle's words and phrases in front of you in a very literal fashion, supported by both traditional and modern commentary.

If we look at a typical Symbol, we can see how this works. Imagine you asked about a new relationship and you received the Symbol *31 Conjoining* as an answer. When you read the Symbol, you will first find the name and a brief set of keywords that give you the essence of what it does.

咸 ䷞ 31 Conjoining HSIEN

Excite, stimulate, influence; strong attraction; bring together what belongs together.

This Symbol describes your situation in terms of the excitement, stimulation and mutual attraction that brings people together, joining what had previously been separated.

You will then see a heading called SETTING THE STAGE. It connects the action in question to a previous action in terms of cause and effect, and urges you to accept this evolution without fear in order to use the energy shown in the current Symbol. It includes a commentary phrase that offers a brief synonym to help you understand the central quality of the new Symbol.

SETTING THE STAGE
From the relations of Heaven and Earth come the myr-iad beings. From the relations of the myriad beings come woman and man, wife and husband, child and parent, server and leader, above and below. Accept this. Do not fear. This is a new beginning. Conjoining means urging things on.

Next, you see the FIELD of meanings that surrounds the name of the Symbol. This gives you a sense of the context in which everything is occurring. You can use any of these meanings to help you understand your problem.

Conjoin, HSIEN: Excite, stimulate, influence, mobilize; strong attraction, connection; bring together what belongs together; make contact; move, trigger; all, totally, universal; unite, conjunction (as planets); liter-ally: a broken piece of pottery, the two halves of which are used to identify partners.

Following the Field comes the RESPONSE, one of the oldest parts of the oracular text, along with a commentary that helps you understand it. This section gives basic advice. It is the direct divinatory response to your question, telling you which actions will bring success in the situation in question.

THE RESPONSE
Conjoining will give you Success and an Advantageous Divination.
Embracing the woman opens the Way.

Conjoining describes your relationship, or your part in it, in terms of a strong attraction, a real influence that triggers you into action. The way to deal with it is to find the best way to bring what is separated back together. This is the energy that brings things together, a sudden attraction, a surge of energy that can create deep connections and lasting relationships. Be open to it and further it. Reach out. Let yourself be moved. Don't be afraid to open up and let the feelings take hold. Embrace the power of the woman and the yin. This generates meaning and good fortune by releasing transformative energy. This attraction can give you a Way to order your heart and everything you are doing.

In some Symbols you will find a notice following this section telling you that this represents a *pivoting phase*, a time when things can change quickly. This indicates that if you want change in your relationship, now is the time to exert your energies.

> This is a pivoting phase, where change can occur quickly and fundamentally. If you want to alter things, apply yourself now.

The section called SYMBOL, REFLECTION AND PRACTICE is based on the analysis of the trigrams and a commentary called Great Symbols that suggests an action typifying a Relating Person's response to the situation. A Relating Person is someone who sees their relationship as a means to live in accord with the Way. This section describes the interaction between the inner and outer worlds by interpreting the qualities of the two trigrams involved and connects it to the nuclear figure hidden at the center of each Symbol to suggest a hidden potential that you may be able to bring out.

This section introduces a reflection and meditative practice that can connect you to the inner meaning of the symbol. The practices are designed to help you relate your experience to love and relationship. This gives you a Way to influence the situation directly through your own inner work and other activities.

SYMBOL, REFLECTION AND PRACTICE

Mists above Mountain. Conjoining. Inner stillness supports stimulation and joy. If you let yourself be led, you can realize hidden potential.

Reflection: The full benefit of men and women together in all combinations is available now. Enjoy as you share. This time is about receptivity to each other, gentle, joyous strength. Look to the woman in your relationship and in yourself for guidance on what is important and how to act. If you seek a relation, take the feminine way. Rather than hunting and seeking, stop and make yourself available to what is coming. Strong forces are moving to bring people together. Act in this Way and the shape of things in your life will change.

Practice: To help you see what to do, regularly imagine that you and your partner are both women, whether or not you are physically. In this imagined relationship, observe the Way both of you live your lives with each other. Ask what advice these two have for you and open yourself completely to their answers.

The final section, **Transforming Lines**, has a different character and purpose. Like the Response, it is from the oldest layers of the text. The Transforming Lines are described in the text as a Nine (transforming yang) or a Six (transforming yin). They show you precisely where change is going on and precisely what the nature of the change is. These lines often provide very specific answers to your question. Each is given with a commentary relating it to your concerns. This is followed by a short statement called *Direction* that shows where the particular line is leading. Read only those lines that are *transforming* in the Primary Symbol that was your answer. If there are no transforming lines, you simply ignore this part of the material.

Let us imagine that you have the fourth line changing in the answer to your question. You would read:

NINE AT FOURTH
> Divination: the Way is open.
> The cause of sorrow disappears.
> You waver back and forth, things come and go.
> Your Friend will simply follow your thoughts.

Express your affection. This is a very favorable influence. Your sorrow over the past will simply disappear. The Way is open. You go back and forth in your thoughts, trying to understand this new feeling. Have no fears. Your Friend will be there for you. *Direction*: Re-imagine the situation. Gather energy for a decisive new move.

Now you are ready to look at the **Relating Symbol**, which shows the way in which you are *related* to the primary situation. You obtain this by changing the transforming lines you obtained in the Primary Symbol into their opposites. The Relating Symbol often shows a potential for the future. But it can also point at an essential quality you need, a goal, a fear or your perspective on the matter at hand. Here you look at only the first parts of the text. If the fourth line of *31 Conjoining* is transforming, it would generate the Relating Symbol *39 Difficulties*. So you would turn to this Symbol and read only the first sections to the end of the Response:

塞 ䷦ 39 *Difficulties/ Limping* CHIEN

Obstacles, afflictions, feeling hampered; overcome difficulties by re-imagining the situation.

SETTING THE STAGE
Turning away inevitably involves hardship. Thus there comes the time of Difficulties. Accept this. Do not fear. Difficulties mean hardship.

OPENING THE FIELD
Difficulty, CHIEN: Obstacles, afflictions, blocks; to feel hampered; overcome difficulties by re-imagining the situation; limp, lame; weak, crooked, unfortunate. The ideogram shows cold feet and suggests a wrong attitude.

THE RESPONSE
Difficulties. The southwest is advantageous.
The northeast is not advantageous.
It is advantageous to see the Great Person.
Divination: the Way is open.

Difficulties describes your relationship, or your part in it, in terms of obstacles and feelings of affliction. The way to deal with it is to see through the difficulties in a new way and gather energy for a decisive new move. You are encountering what feels like an endless set of obstacles. Nothing is going right. You don't really have the strength to confront all this. Well, don't. Stop trying to be a hero. Retreat, pull back, open yourself to other people. Don't go on struggling alone. Talk to someone who can help you reflect on this situation. This generates meaning and good fortune by releasing transformative energy. It is the way you are thinking about things that makes it all so hard.

There is danger all around you. If you can see it and stop pushing on, you will understand what is happening. Correct the way you use power and change what you depend on. Re-imagine this situation. Then you will link your relationship with something great.

From this we might think that the person asking the question will soon encounter difficulties in their relationship that will demand a new way of looking at things. We could also link this to the wavering quality described in the Transforming Line of the Primary Symbol and conclude that their current attitude toward the situation was actually creating these difficulties. By fully yielding to the attraction they were feeling, the situation would soon become clear.

A Quick Guide to Using the Oracle

- Make a clear question. The clearer the question, the clearer to answer. Make it about something important to your feeling life. Decide who you are as an inquirer: do you ask as someone seeking love or someone who is part of an existing relationship. Decide what this question means to you.
- Set off a quiet, calm place where you can pose the question and reflect on the answer.
- Use one of the methods described on pages 22–25 to generate the six lines of the Primary Symbol. There are four possible kinds of lines:

9 ——⊖——	8 —— ——	6 ——✕——	7 ————
old yang	**young yin**	**old yin**	**young yang**
transforms into >		*transforms into >*	

- Record the lines starting from the bottom up. If any of the lines are transforming, change them in order to generate the Relating Figure:

```
6 [          ]                           [          ]
5 [          ]    Outer Trigram          [          ]
4 [          ]                           [          ]

3 [          ]                           [          ]
2 [          ]    Inner Trigram          [          ]
1 [          ]                           [          ]
```

Primary Figure   *transforms to:*   **Relating Figure**

Number: _____   Number: _____
Name: _____   Name: _____

- Use the *Key to the Symbols* on page 308–309 to identify the number and name of both of your Symbols.
- Read all the basic texts of the Primary Figure and the special text attached to any line that is *transforming*. Then read the first three sections of the Relating Figure (Setting the Stage, Opening the Field, The Response and its commentary). Decide how this relates you to the Primary Figure: is it the future, a desired goal, something you want to avoid, a basic concern? You will probably feel an immediate intuitive connection to the answer. Keep that in mind as you explore all the possibilities, the way the words explain your situation, "turning and rolling the words in your heart".

THE 64
SYMBOLS OF LOVE

Part I: Foundations

Part I of *Symbols of Love* is the Book of Foundations. It begins with the Primal Powers, Father Heaven and Mother Earth. It moves through several pivotal phases: the interaction of Heaven and Earth (Symbols 11 and 12); the disappearance and reappearance of spirit (Symbols 23 and 24); and the emergence of water and fire, the opposites that characterize life on Earth (Symbols 29 and 30).

Each of these above Symbols represents a place where things can change quickly and fundamentally. These are the times to apply yourself if you want to alter your relationship, for better or for worse. In the text, the Symbols are indicated by a box:

This is a pivoting phase, where change can occur quickly and fundamentally. If you want to alter your relationship, apply yourself now.

乾 ䷀ 1 *Force* CH'IEN

Creative energy; persist, create, endure; power to guide and inspire, dynamic and enduring.

SETTING THE STAGE
Your relationship stems from the Way and the One. It is self-generating. Accept this. Do not fear. Force means being strong.

OPENING THE FIELD
Force, CH'IEN: spirit, creative energy, action, inspiration, masculine drive; activate, animate, command and guide; strong, tenacious, untiring, firm, stable; *also*: destroy, dry up, exhaust, clear away, clean out. The ideogram shows the graphs for the One and above.

Force is one of the Eight Helping Spirits. He is the strong one. He awes and wars in the Heavens. As a spirit guide, Force is tireless creative energy, shape-changing, relentless, riding a Dragon, inspiring, creating dynamic harmony. He is dangerous. He is a tiger. He brings deep abiding joy.

THE RESPONSE
> **Force will give you Fundamental Success and an Advantageous Divination.**

Force describes your relationship, or your part in it, in terms of the primal power of spirit to create and destroy. The way to deal with it is to persist and to inspire. It is time to create the deep connections. You are the active, inspiring part. You have the capacity to guide the course of your relationship and bring out its purpose. Though you are confronted with many obstacles, do not fear. The fundamental creative energy is there and you can use it. Be dynamic, tenacious and untiring. Success will be yours in the end.

SYMBOL, REFLECTION AND PRACTICE

Heaven moves and persists. The entire situation contains a great creative potential. Its images are the power of Heaven, the light of the sun causing all things to grow, the fertilizing rain, the creative energy of the dragon.

Reflection: Whatever is going on is filled with creative force. Success is assured if you persist. You and your Friend are sharing this creativity already. Use it to build your strength with each other. Heaven is blessing your fundamental connection with one another. Look for the creativity in your Friend. Claim it for yourselves and celebrate it together. Express it through overt acts. Facing and resolving challenges together will strengthen your basic connection. Yang energy is strong now. Both men and women need to learn to share this with each other.

Practice: Sit quietly for a few minutes each day. Concentrate on what is physically supporting you until you are well grounded. Then imagine that brilliant, vibrant, harmonious spiritual energy is streaming into you from all sides. It goes straight to your heart. There it turns and streams out of you in all directions. The whole cycle is self-supporting and continual. You become a star source of creative energy.

Transforming Lines

INITIAL NINE
Immersed dragon, don't use it!

The relationship feels confused and uncertain. You would like to take hold and set it right. Don't do it. Not yet. The creative energy is still under water. But have no fear. It will soon emerge. *Direction*: Have no doubts. You are coupled with a creative force.

NINE AT SECOND
> **See the dragon in the field!**
> **It is advantageous to see the Great Person.**

Creative energy emerges into the field of the relationship. You have the ability to realize things now. Take the advice of people you know and trust. Reflect on what you and your Friend really want from a relationship. See what is great in yourselves and your love. *Direction:* Bring people together. Give them a goal. You are coupled with a creative force.

NINE AT THIRD
> **The Relating Person completes the day,**
> **using Force again and again.**
> **At night come alarms and adversity.**
> **This is not a mistake.**

This is a time of incessant activity. The relationship is plagued by practical and emotional problems. Old ghosts come back to haunt you. Don't worry. This is a transition. Turn your back on your past and commit yourself wholly to this relationship. It marks the return of the Way in your life. *Direction:* Make your Way step by step. Find supportive people. Gather energy for a decisive new move.

NINE AT FOURTH
> **Perhaps playing in the whirlpools.**
> **This is not a mistake.**

Even though the two of you are dealing with big emotional issues, don't lose the playful spirit. Joy is the key to creative energy in this situation. Don't get frozen into a single stance. *Direction:* Accumulate Small things to build the great. Turn conflict into creative tension. The situation is already changing.

NINE AT FIFTH

Flying dragon in the Heavens.
It is advantageous to see the Great Person.

Spread your wings. Let your love be felt. Your Friend will recognize your energy and guidance. Now is the time to build a creative, enduring relationship, a permanent bond. Listen to people you know and trust. Seek out what is great in yourself and see how it is reflected in your Friend and the bond between you. *Direction*: This begins a fertile time, rich with warmth and light. Be resolute. You are connected with a creative force.

NINE ABOVE

Overbearing dragon, there will be cause for sorrow.

You are trying to order your Friend around and dominate the relation rather than inspire it. This is a misuse of the creative energy you have been given. If you go on like this, you will certainly have something to be sorry about. Why not stop now? *Direction*: Resolve to do better. Act differently. You are connected to a creative force.

坤 ䷁ *2 Field* KUN

Yield, nourish, provide for; gentle, receptive, welcoming; give all things form.

SETTING THE STAGE

This relationship stems from the Way and the One. It is self-generating. Accept this. Do not fear. Field means being supple.

OPENING THE FIELD

Field, KUN: the Earth on which all things rest, the world, concrete existence, the power to give things form and existence; moon, mother, wife, servants, ministers; supple, adaptable, receptive, yielding; welcome, consent, respond to, agree, follow; give birth to, bear fruit; nourish, provide for, serve, work. The ideogram portrays the spirits of the Earth.

Field is one of the Eight Helping Spirits. She is the compliant one. She is offered service at the Earth Altar. As a spirit guide, Field opens, yields and receives all things into her. She is the flow, the provider, welcome everywhere, the opening that receives the seed of Sky. Her hands give blessings. She receives the dead. She is the mare roaming the Earth tirelessly.

THE RESPONSE

Field will give Fundamental Success
and an Advantageous Divination to the mare.
The Relating Person should have a direction to go.
At first there will be illusion, then you acquire what
you desire.
It is advantageous to find a lord.
You acquire partners in the Southwest.
You lose partners in the Northeast.
Divination: quiet understanding opens the Way.

Field describes your relationship, or your part in it, in terms of the primal power to nourish and give things form. The way to deal with this situation is to yield to each thing, providing what it needs to exist. This hexagram is about creating a relationship. You are in a position to nourish your relationship and ground it in what is real. You are confronted with many conflicting demands. Be like the mare, receptive and tireless, and the field will open up. Simply yield to each thing in turn and give it what it needs. Don't try to impose your will. Keep your purpose in mind—the creation of an enduring connection. If you want it, you will be successful and open up a whole new time. At first you may be confused by everything that is going on, but you will soon understand what needs to be done. Work in a supporting position. Let your Friend take the lead. Common activities and goals strengthen the relationship; solitary striving weakens it. The Way opens to your love through quiet understanding and acceptance.

SYMBOL, REFLECTION AND PRACTICE

Power of Earth. Field. The entire situation contains a great formative potential. Its images are the Earth, the moon, the mother, the devoted servant, the mare.

Reflection: Cherish your Friend with openness and receptivity. Offer yourself softly. Sit together regularly. Notice your Friend keenly through the sensations stimulated in you as you open your awareness to them. Avoid going outside yourself for this intimacy. The deepest connection comes through your own sensations. Yin energy is strong now and both men and women need to express this. The seeds of the relationship that you want are sown. Nurture them and give them a chance to grow. Support each other. Contribute to what you share by doing your part. Acceptance is the key in everything. Let things unfold.

Practice: Sit each day imagining that your Friend is nestled in your heart. Accept, embrace, love and nurture your Friend there. He or she thrives in the primal nourishment of your heart energy.

Transforming Lines

INITIAL SIX
Treading the frost culminates in hardening the ice.

Your relationship is beginning to solidify and take form out of the watery mass of feelings. Act slowly, carefully and persistently to build a base. *Direction*: Something very important is returning. Be open and provide what is needed.

SIX AT SECOND
Straight, on all sides and Great.
No need to repeat or rehearse.
There is nothing for which this will not be advantageous.

The time is ripe for this relationship. Commit yourself fully. Go right to the point. You don't have to plan or rehearse anything. Everything is there. This connection will benefit everything in your life. *Direction*: Organize your forces. This is the return of something great. Be open and provide what is needed.

SIX AT THIRD
Divination: a containing beauty,
an order that makes things possible.
If perhaps you are an adherent of a King's affairs,
The time of no accomplishments comes to an end.

Act together through a design that contains and conceals. This is the place of hidden excellence. Contain your feelings and desires. You can bring all your plans to a beautiful completion. Think of what is distant. This is a far-reaching time with far-reaching effects. *Direction*: Keep your words clear and close to the facts. Release bound energy. The situation is already changing.

Six at Fourth

Bundled in the bag.
Without mistakes, without praise.

The relationship is in the bag, pregnant with possibilities. There is nothing to blame or praise. What you want is already there. Careful consideration is advantageous. *Direction*: Build reserves of strength for future joy. Re-imagine the situation. Gather energy for a decisive new move.

Six at Fifth

A yellow lower garment.
The Way to the Source is open.

There are hidden processes at work in your relationship that open the way to an enduring connection. Accept them, even though things may look confusing. Have patience and trust. What is happening now will affect you both deeply and positively. This will be the source of great good fortune and meaningful events. *Direction*: Change your group. Strip away your old ideas. Be open and provide what is needed.

Six Above

Dragons struggle in the countryside.
Their blood flows indigo and yellow.

In a struggle between the Sky power and the Earth power, both are injured. It needn't be this way. Don't try to assert your power now. Yield, give way, restore the peace. Do not try to dominate the relationship. *Direction*: Strip away your old ideas. Be open and provide what is needed.

屯 ䷂ *3 Sprouting* CHUN

**Begin, establish, found; gather your strength,
surmount difficulties.**

SETTING THE STAGE
First there were Heaven and Earth. Now the myriad beings are
born. Sprouting. Truly, the myriad beings fill the space between
Heaven and Earth to overflowing. This is the time of the Great.
Accept this. Do not fear. Sprouting means to fill things to overflowing. Sprouting means that the beginning of all being is
giving birth. Sprouting means being seen but not letting go of
your residence. Make your influence felt afar.

OPENING THE FIELD
Sprout, CHUN: begin to grow; assemble, accumulate, amass; establish a base of operations; difficult, arduous, painful; all the
difficulties at the beginning of an endeavor. The ideogram shows
a plant breaking through the Earth.

THE RESPONSE
> **Sprouting will give you Fundamental Success
> and an Advantageous Divination.
> Do not use having a direction to go.
> Advantageous to install helpers.**

Sprouting describes your relationship, or your part in it, in terms
of beginning growth. The way to deal with it is to assemble
things and accumulate energy together for a difficult yet exciting
task. This relationship is just beginning to grow, like a young
plant breaking through the covering Earth. It is the tenderness of
the sprout, so easy to crush yet capable of pushing through rock-
hard ground, the inexorable power of the yielding path that

reaches out towards Heaven. You don't yet know where this will go. Assemble the energy and provide the care for a long, hard, joyous effort. If you can accept the time and the work this will take, it can open a whole new world. There are many new things emerging now. You will find out quite a bit about yourself, your Friend and the surprising possibilities of this relationship. Involve other people in the opening up of your relationship. Don't try to impose your ideas or force affection into a preconceived pattern. Get rid of old experiences and let what is really there come into view. There is work to be done, to be able to respond to this surprising gift from fate.

SYMBOL, REFLECTION AND PRACTICE
Clouds and Thunder. Sprouting. The old time is ending, while a new time is sprouting within. This is the time to strip away old ideas and experiences.

Reflection: Things have begun to grow, however they are still fragile and tender. Give yourselves time to get used to being together in ways that nurture the new developments. Deliberately make time to do this. If you try to force things, you could do damage. This is a time for receptive sharing, not a time for filling your lives with things to do. Make preparations for furthering what is emerging now. Let go of expectations and change old patterns. Stay with what is, rather than getting ahead of it. The sprout is not fully grown. It will grow if gently nurtured.

Practice: Spend time each day paying close attention to yourself in your surroundings. Use all five senses to connect physically to what is around you. Notice your inner physical experiences. Let go of fantasy, memory, thought and feeling. Stay with the physical. Notice how you become increasingly rooted in the world and notice the energy that flows through you as you do.

Transforming Lines

Initial Nine

> **Sprouting. A stone pillar.**
> **Divination: Staying where you are is advantageous.**
> **Advantageous to install helpers.**

Stop and establish the foundations for this relationship. Connect this experience to your own deep roots. Involve your Friend. Don't be secretive about your love. You are on the right track. *Direction*: Find supportive friends. Group with people for mutual support. Strip away old ideas. Provide what is needed.

Six at Second

> **First sprouting then quitting,**
> **riding your horse in full array.**
> **That person you see isn't an outlaw, seek a marriage.**
> **Divination: the woman will not yet nurse a child.**
> **After ten years she will nurse one.**

You reach out to people, then turn away from them. You are all prepared for an emotional encounter but see your Friend as an outlaw. Drop the hostility. Seek a permanent connection. It will be a while before this connection bears fruit, but in the end it will all come right. *Direction*: Articulate your needs and desires. Take in the past. Provide what is needed.

Six at Third

> **Following a stag without guides or precautions,**
> **You wander into the center of the forest.**
> **The Relating Person almost fails to realize**
> **what is happening.**
> **Going on like this brings distress and confusion.**

You are losing yourself in the difficulties at the beginning of this relationship, following your impulses and desires without a second thought. You are right on the edge of disaster. If you want this relation to go on, stop now before you lose sight of what is really worthwhile. *Direction*: The situation is already changing.

SIX AT FOURTH

Riding a horse in full array.
Seek a marriage vow from the one you love.
Going on opens the Way.
There is nothing for which this will not be
advantageous.

The time is right. The difficulties are over. Make the connection. Pledge your love in front of the community. This will be of great benefit to everyone concerned. *Direction*: Follow this flow of events. Proceed step by step. Gather energy for a decisive new move.

NINE AT FIFTH

Sprouting, you have its juice.
Divination: Small opens the Way.
Divination: Great closes the Way.

This is the essence of growth, the flowing sap or juice. It brings things to life, it spreads the wealth. You have this source of vital growth in your relationship now. Be careful with it. Make sure everything gets what it needs. Don't impose your will on your Friend. *Direction*: Something important is re-entering your life. Be open to it. Provide what is needed.

SIX ABOVE

Riding a horse in full array
While weeping blood courses down.
Why let this go on?

This is a disastrous way to relate to each other. It is doing you very real harm, bleeding you in literal and emotional ways. Don't think you can simply fix it. You must let go of the situation now before it gets worse. *Direction*: A better time is coming. Strip away your old ideas and be open to new ones. Provide what is needed.

蒙 ䷃ 4 Enveloping/ Ignorance MENG

Immature, unaware, foolish; hidden, concealed; nurture hidden growth.

SETTING THE STAGE

Something being born must be enveloped. Thus there comes the time of Enveloping. Accept this. Do not fear. Enveloping means being enveloped. It means that something is immature and needs to be nourished. Its disorder is conspicuous.

OPENING THE FIELD

Envelop, MENG: cover, hide, conceal; dull, unaware, ignorant, foolish, uneducated, undeveloped; young, fragile; unseen beginnings. The ideogram suggests nurturing hidden growth.

THE RESPONSE

Enveloping will give you Success.
"I do not seek the ignorant youth, the ignorant
youth seeks me."
At the first consultation there is information.
By asking two or three times, things are simply obscured.
When things are obscured, there is no information.
This is an Advantageous Divination!

Enveloping describes your relationship, or your part in it, in terms of hidden meaning and lack of awareness. The way to deal with it is to accept being hidden in order to nurture further growth. You don't know what you are doing or why you are doing it at the moment. There is much concealed from you. If you try to push things you will simply spread embarrassment and confusion. Stay concealed for now. Give things a chance to grow. Accept being hidden to nurture the growing power of awareness and real affection. You and your Friend have been asking the same question over and over again. The answer is already there, if you will only see it. What you see as an obstacle to your happiness is protecting its inner growth. When you really understand this, you will be ready for the relationship. That is why the situation is so advantageous.

SYMBOL, REFLECTION AND PRACTICE
Below Mountain, a Spring. Enveloping. The outer obstruction hides and protects inner change. Deep sources of energy are returning in this hidden growth.

Reflection: Practice restraint. Identify what you already know together and strengthen it. It is important to both think and feel, not just do what your impulses prompt you to do. You will learn and mature in ways that will enrich your capacity to be with someone. Anguishing over the same questions does not usually produce helpful answers. Withhold action until the wisest course is very obvious. Avoid acting impulsively with each other. Consider the likely consequences to yourself and to others, before you say or do anything.

Practice: Throughout the day, whenever you have an impulse to do something, pause. Then ground yourself thoroughly by paying close attention to what is physically supporting you—the floor, the ground, a seat. Do something only when your impulse to act has dissolved.

Transforming Lines

INITIAL SIX
Far-reaching enveloping.
Though it is advantageous to punish people,
Loosen the fetters and shackles on the youth.
Going on like this brings distress and confusion.

You have to correct a far-reaching error before you can enjoy contact with your Friend. Be clear and discriminating with the people around you. Free the youthful energy that you are now confining. Simply going on will cover you with distress and confusion. *Direction*: Decrease passionate involvement. Return to the source of your affection. Be open and provide what is needed.

NINE AT SECOND

> **Enwrapped and enveloped. The Way opens.**
> **Let a wife in. The Way is open.**
> **This young son can control the dwelling.**

Here being hidden and enveloped turns into caring for and protecting your Friend. It is time to take a wife and establish a family dwelling. You have the ability to do this and the time is right. *Direction*: Strip away your old ideas and be open to the new. Provide what is needed.

SIX AT THIRD

> **Do not connect with this grasping woman!**
> **She sees a husband made of precious metal**
> **who has no body.**
> **There is no advantageous direction.**

You are flirting with someone malicious and selfish, interested only in wealth and power. If you become involved you will lose your independence and your capacity to express yourself. There is nothing of value here. Beware! *Direction*: Renovate a corrupt relationship. If you let yourself be led, you can realize hidden potential. The change is already underway.

SIX AT FOURTH

> **Confining Envelopment. Distress and confusion.**

This isn't nurturing hidden growth. You are locking yourself in a prison. You don't have to confine your expressions of affection and your insights so rigidly. This just leads to distress and confusion. You are cutting yourself off from your Friend. *Direction*: Gather energy for a decisive new move.

SIX AT FIFTH

Young enveloping. The Way is open.

This is the perfect way to deal with the situation. You have accepted your immaturity and the fact that there is something hidden in the situation. All will go well. The Way will open and will lead you to real connection with your Friend and a real understanding. Be patient and have faith. *Direction*: Disperse obstacles to understanding. Take things in. Be open and provide what is needed.

NINE ABOVE

Attacking the enveloping.
It is not advantageous to act like an outlaw.
It is advantageous to resist being an outlaw.

You are fighting against the very processes that, in the long run, will give you what you need. Change your attitude toward your Friend. Don't run around making demands. Resist the temptation to act impulsively. Use this time to organize yourself. Then the fruit literally falls into your hand. *Direction*: Return to the source of your affection. Be open and provide what is needed.

需 ䷄ 5 Attending HSÜ

Wait for, wait on, attend to what is needed; wait for the right moment.

SETTING THE STAGE

When something is immature you must nourish it. Thus there comes the time of Attending. Accept this. Do not fear. Attending means the way of eating and drinking. Attending means not pushing yourself forward.

OPENING THE FIELD

Attend, HSÜ: take care of something, serve, provide what is needed; necessary, need; call for; wait for, have patience; stopped by rain and the ability to make rain. The ideogram shows the source of rain.

RESPONSE

Attending will give you a connection to the spirits and shining Success.
Divination: the Way is open.
Advantageous to step into the Great River.

Attending describes your relationship, or your part in it, in terms of waiting for and serving. You need patience, perception and care. You must wait for things to develop and you must wait on things, giving what your Friend and the situation need. Wait for the right moment to act. If you can combine these two kinds of waiting the spirits will give you a brilliant success and an enduring connection. The love you long for will be yours and you will be able to count on it as you step into the Great River of Life together. It will be a source of nourishment for all.

SYMBOL, REFLECTION AND PRACTICE

Clouds above Heaven. Attending. Creative energy confronts danger through attention and waiting. You can turn what looks like discord into real creative tension.

Reflection: Enjoy your times of aloneness and togetherness. Things are working well. Timing is still important, so avoid jumping in prematurely. Be sensitive to each other's needs. Do things to celebrate life together. What you want with your Friend is close at hand. Find ways to nourish what you cherish in yourself and to nourish what you want to share. However, while the time is ripe with potential, it is not yet right. Keep exchanging with each other. Persevere with your plans and wait for the right moment to act.

Practice: Take time each day to practice waiting patiently. Sit still and attend to the beauty, love, joy, fragrance and harmony that fills and surrounds you. Notice how this increasingly fills a reservoir with these energies for your future.

Transforming Lines

INITIAL NINE

> **Attending on the outskirts.**
> **It is advantageous to persevere.**
> **This is not a mistake.**

It feels like your Friend is far away. You can't make contact. But underneath, the connection is certainly there. Persevere! Don't lose patience. You are not making a mistake. *Direction*: Stay connected to the source of your values. Turn conflict into creative tension. The situation is already changing.

NINE AT SECOND

> **Attending on the sands.**
> **There is Small talk.**
> **Completing this opens the Way.**

You are becoming a bit closer to your Friend, but the social situation keeps shifting. All around you people are chattering. Don't worry. They can't hurt you. Keep your eye on what is important and go through this. The Way is opening from the center of this. *Direction:* The situation is already changing.

NINE AT THIRD

Attending in the bogs.
This will attract outlaws in the end.

You have become bogged down in negative feelings. You have lost the sense of attending or waiting on something precious. This leaves you vulnerable to attack and risks the loss of your relationship. There is still time, so think it over. What did you do to create this unfortunate situation? *Direction:* Set limits and articulate things. Take things in. Be open and provide what is needed.

SIX AT FOURTH

Attending in blood.
Get out of the cave where this begins!

You and your relationship are in immediate danger. Whatever you are doing, stop! Get out of the place where you are trapped. You can save things now if you will only listen. *Direction:* Be resolute. Take action. You are connected to a creative force.

NINE AT FIFTH

Attending, drinking liquor and eating.
Divination: the Way opens.

You make the connection. Let pleasure, harmony and peace open the Way between you. The spirits will be present. This cheer brings you out of your isolation. *Direction:* A fertile time is approaching. If you let yourself be led, you can realize hidden potential. The situation is already changing.

SIX ABOVE

> Enter the cave. Visitors will come without urging.
> There are three people coming: Respect them.
> Bringing this to completion opens the Way.

Though you are trying your best to work with the relationship, you do not really know what to do. Don't worry. Go into your center of energy. There are three unannounced visitors on the way who will show you. Respect them and the way to happiness will suddenly open. *Direction*: Accumulate the Small to achieve the great. Turn conflict into creative tension. The situation is already changing.

訟 ䷅ 6 Arguing SUNG

Conflict, quarrels, arguments; express what you feel; resolve or retreat from conflict.

SETTING THE STAGE
When there is eating and drinking together, people will surely argue. Thus there comes the time of Arguing. Accept this. Do not fear. Arguing means not connecting.

OPENING THE FIELD
Argue, SUNG: quarrels, wrangles, controversy, disagreement; dispute, plead your case, state your position; contend in front of a judge, arrive at a judgement, resolve a conflict; lodge a complaint, litigate, reprimand. The ideogram shows pleading before an authority.

THE RESPONSE

Arguing gives you a connection to the spirits.

Restrain your alarm.

Centering yourself opens the Way.

Completing the conflict closes the Way.

It is advantageous to see the Great Person.

It is not advantageous to step into the Great River.

Arguing describes your relationship, or your part in it, in terms of conflict and dispute. The way to deal with it is to express your viewpoint clearly, but retreat from aggressive action or escalating anger. You and your Friend are quarreling. Don't be alarmed. Be careful. Express yourself clearly and calmly without taking aggressive action. If you can't get your point across, then retreat from the conflict. These are deep waters. Don't be carried away by anger or passion. Stay centered. If you try to carry the argument to the bitter end you will regret it. See people you both respect. Get an outside opinion.

SYMBOL, REFLECTION AND PRACTICE

Heaven and Stream, contradicting movement. Arguing. With no solid inner base, you must express your feelings through words. Through this you can find the intimacy and connection of people living together in a dwelling.

Reflection: If you handle your situation well, the conflict will strengthen you and your connections with each other. Remember that any conflict with others shows that you have the same conflict within yourself. Your Friend is reflecting an aspect of you. Your inner conflict is the one to resolve. Find ways to express clearly what is important to you. Stay true to this without compromise, while staying open to your Friend's position. Avoid attack or abuse of any sort. Sharing problems and strong feelings is an intense form of intimacy. It can strengthen your relationship with each other. Persevere and practice patience. Trying to force a result may create unnecessary conflict. Seeking counsel and guidance from someone outside the situation will help.

Practice: Spend time each day considering at least three things that your Friend is doing or expressing with which you disagree. Take each one in turn and, while alone, do or express these in the same way as your Friend does. Own these things as if they are truly yours. Notice carefully how things change for the better in your relationship.

Transforming Lines

INITIAL SIX
**This is not the place to be perpetually active.
There is Small talk. Bring this to completion and the
Way opens.**

This is not where you and you Friend need to be, always discussing trivial affairs. Be done with it. The Way is open to you. *Direction*: Proceed step by step. Find supportive friends. Gather energy for a decisive new move.

NINE AT SECOND

> **Don't try to control this situation through arguing.**
> **Change your plans and escape to your capital,**
> **to your people's three hundred doors.**
> **Without error.**

You cannot win this fight, so change your plans. Go back to your own people, where the doors are open to you, even if you must sneak away. This is not a mistake. When the distress comes to an end, your Friend will seek you out. *Direction*: Communication is blocked. Proceed step by step. Gather energy for a decisive new move.

SIX AT THIRD

> **Eating the ancient power and virtue.**
> **Divination: going through the adversity opens the Way.**
> **If you are an adherent of a King's affairs, they will**
> **not be accomplished.**

To deal with this situation you need the power and the insight of the ancient sages. You and your Friend are facing a horde of angry ghosts, things from the past that are returning to haunt you. Take heart and fight your way through together, even though your social and business duties may suffer. *Direction*: This is a fated encounter. It connects you with a creative force.

NINE AT FOURTH

> **Do not seek to control this situation through arguing.**
> **Simply return to yourself, fate is approaching.**
> **Divination: self-denial and quiet open the Way.**

You cannot win this fight, so change your plans. Return to yourself, disengage from the conflict. Fate is approaching now and will completely change the situation. Deny yourself the luxury of violent or acrimonious feelings. Stay quiet, accepting and peaceful. This is a crucial moment. Don't let go of this chance. *Direction*: Clear up obstacles to understanding. Take things in. Be open to the new and provide what is needed.

NINE AT FIFTH
Through arguing the Way to the Source is open.

Now is the time to convince your Friend of the reality of the love between you. State your case with clarity and confidence and expect positive results. This will resolve the situation and open the Way to a much better time. *Direction*: Gather energy for a decisive new move.

NINE ABOVE
**Arguing, perhaps a pouched belt is bestowed on you.
Complete dawn three times and you
will be deprived of it.**

You are contesting for mastery in this relationship. If you think you can win this way, then please think again quickly. Anything you gain will soon vanish and you will be left alone. This really is not worthy of you. It will bring you no respect at all. *Direction*: Break out of isolation. Find supportive friends. Gather energy for a decisive new move.

師 ䷆ *7 Legions/Leader* SHIH

Organize, mobilize, lead; armies and soldiers; a master craftsman, martial arts master; discipline, power.

SETTING THE STAGE

When people argue they rise up like disorganized crowds. Thus there comes the time of Legions and the Leader. Accept this. Do not fear. Legions means organizing crowds. Legions means dealing with grief.

OPENING THE FIELD

Legions/leader, SHIH: troops, an army; master, leader, general; master at arms, master craftsman; organize, make functional, mobilize; educate, order, discipline; imitate, take as a model. The ideogram shows people moving around a common center.

THE RESPONSE

> **Legions. Divination: experienced people open the Way.**
> **This is not a mistake.**

Legions describes your relationship, or your part in it, in terms of turning a confused heap of things into functional units so you can take effective action and find a joint purpose. The way to deal with it is to first organize your thoughts and your feelings. This is a time to put yourself and your relationship in order. Focus on your needs and problems. You have some housekeeping and clarifying to do. Work on the capacity to lead, to see clearly and act directly. Talk to people who have experience in the things that bring you together. This generates meaning and good fortune by releasing transformative energy. This is the time of the soldier and the leader. But the ideal of this army is to protect people who cannot protect themselves, to serve and civilize.

SYMBOL, REFLECTION AND PRACTICE

Stream in the Earth. Danger. Legions. A willingness to take risks and the desire to serve are what make the Legions powerful. Go back to the beginning. A powerful energy is returning.

Reflection: This is a time to get organized with each other, to arrange practicalities and work out roles. Figure out what is needed to achieve the things you value and arrange to do it. Meet regularly. Make lists of what needs to be done. Face the need to act decisively. This could involve one of you as leader and the other as supporter. Confront your own issues about taking the lead when there is need. Remember as you face potential divisiveness that it is your own strengths and weaknesses that you are seeing. Support each other through the process. There is a way through what you are facing.

Practice: Start each day by sitting and considering the important things you need to complete that day. Imagine that you are at the end of the day and that all your jobs are completed. Imagine that they were completed easily and well. Celebrate this. Then go and do what is necessary.

Transforming Lines

INITIAL SIX

**Legions issuing forth must use regulations.
But obstructing their real power and virtue closes
the Way.**

Everything needs rules and regulations, even relationships. Without them, your love, your energy and your enthusiasm will disintegrate and you will accomplish nothing. But be sure the rules you set for yourself are not obstructing your real power. *Direction:* A stimulating influence approaches. Something important returns. Be open and provide what is needed.

NINE AT SECOND

Located in the center of the legions. The Way is open.
This is not a mistake.
The King bestows a mandate three times.

You are in the leader's position, at the center of a well-organized relationship. The Way is open to you. You have corrected your faults. Now you receive a mandate to act and you are in a position to carry out your mutual plans and desires. Make no mistake. This is an honor. Carrying this through will change your life. *Direction*: Be open. Provide what is needed.

SIX AT THIRD

Perhaps the legions are carting corpses.
The Way closes.

Dead bodies, old memories, useless ideas and false images of what you want surround your relationship. You must get rid of them. You must do it now. *Direction*: Make the effort. If you let yourself be led, you can realize hidden potential. The situation is already changing.

SIX AT FOURTH

Legions rest on the left, the side of peace.
This is not a mistake.

Your conflict with your Friend, and with the world you both live in, is dissolving. Be open. Don't be defensive. Value this peace. It is not a mistake. *Direction*: Release bound energy. The situation is already changing.

SIX AT FIFTH

The birds of prey take to the fields.
It is advantageous to hold onto your words.
This is not a mistake.

> **If the elder son conducts the legions**
> **While the younger son must cart the corpses,**
> **Divination: the Way closes.**

Conflict has broken out and you must engage whether you like it or not. Keep hold of your tongue and you will avoid mistakes. It is very important that you do not simply take the upper hand and leave the dirty work to your Friend. If you do that your cause is lost. Take responsibility yourself. Above all, get rid of your old ideas, irrelevant images and bad memories. *Direction*: Take decisive action. Take risks. Be open and provide what is needed.

Six Above

> **The Great Leader receives the mandate.**
> **Lay out the city and receive the dwellers.**
> **Do not use Small People.**

You have succeeded in more ways than one. You have turned yourself into a leader and you have received a mandate from your Friend to establish a base where the two of you can dwell. Use all your powers to create a beautiful place. Receive other people as a part of your relationship. If you let them into the city of your heart, make sure there is a reason for them to be there. Have no fear. Simply do what you have to do. *Direction*: The situation contains hidden possibilities. Something important is returning. Be open and provide what is needed.

比 ䷇ 8 *Grouping* PI

Mutual support, spiritual kin; change how you think about things and who you are grouped with.

SETTING THE STAGE
Crowds must have a place to group. Thus there comes the time of Grouping. Accept this. Do not fear. Grouping means groups. Grouping means taking delight in things and people.

OPENING THE FIELD
Group, PI: join together, ally; spiritual connections; find a new center, join a new group; find what you belong with; order things in classes, compare and select; harmonize, unite, equal, identical; work together, work towards, neighbors. The ideogram shows someone who stops and looks around.

THE RESPONSE

Grouping opens the Way.
Use the oracle again and again
to connect with the perpetual Source.
This is not a mistake.
This will not be a soothing time,
things are coming on all sides.
For the husband who is late the Way closes.

Grouping describes your relationship, or your part in it, in terms of the people and things with whom your spirit connects you. The way to deal with it is examine where and how you support and are supported by people and ideas. The situation is presenting you and your Friend with a challenge. Stop and think deeply about the way you see things and people with whom you are connected. The way you are grouped can be a heartfelt bond, a spiritual connection that provides great mutual support. You may have to change yours. Take the time to look at things carefully. Why did you ask the question you asked? Rise to the challenge, to understand how and why you group things and people. Use the oracle to help you sort things out. This generates meaning and good fortune by releasing transformative energy. Make no mistake, this is not a soothing time. It is a very important transition. Above all, move now and move sincerely. If not, you will soon be a prospective suitor without a partner or a Friend in sight.

SYMBOL, REFLECTION AND PRACTICE

Stream above Earth. Grouping. The outer world dissolves while new relations appear on the inner field. Now is the time to strip away your outmoded ideas and experiences.

Reflection: Relationships change constantly. Sometimes the changes are fundamental. Now is a time to review your allegiances and what you are doing about them. The challenges you are facing can strengthen your relationship. Resolution usually comes as each person resolves his or her own issues by claiming the things that they admire in the other as also being their own. Be prepared to let go of old expectations, patterns and relationships. Allow yourself to change. This might require the severing of old connections. Keep things as enjoyable and happy as you can. Affirm and draw on your own qualities as a person. This is a time for action. You are facing it precisely because you are now ready to deal with it.

Practice: Sit still and quietly each day for a few minutes. Bring into your awareness the people and groups that surround you. Imagine them entering your heart and dwelling there. Face whatever reactions and experiences that are stimulated by accepting their presence in you. Do this by relaxing your body as much as you can. Avoid analysis and notice any spontaneous insights you have.

Transforming Lines

INITIAL SIX
> There is a connection to the spirits in this grouping.
> This is not a mistake.
> This connection to the spirits fills the jar
> to overflowing.
> In the completion that is coming,
> There is even more of a connection to the spirits.

Joining your Friend, becoming part of the group, will connect you with the flow of the spirit. This is certain. There is no mistake here. This group overflows with love and care. As you become part of it, you will find there is more on the way. *Direction*: Give everything a place to grow. Strip away old ideas and be open to new ones.

SIX AT SECOND
> Inside the origin of the group.
> Divination: the Way is open.

Your connection with your Friend puts you at the center of this group. You are a part of its origin. The Way is open to you. Don't let this connection slip through your fingers. *Direction*: Commit yourself. Take risks. Be open to the new and provide what is needed.

SIX AT THIRD
> A group of people who have no value to you.

Either your Friend or the people you are involved with will do you no good. These are the wrong people for you. Leave now before they do you harm. *Direction*: Re-imagine the situation. Gather energy for a decisive new move.

SIX AT FOURTH
> **Outside the group. Divination: the Way is open.**

You are outside the group that your Friend seems to be a part of. Don't let this bother you. You are in this position because of your moral and intellectual worth. Stick to your work and your values. The Way is open. *Direction*: Assemble things for a great new project. Proceed through gentle penetration. Gather energy for a decisive new move.

NINE AT FIFTH
> **A manifestation of true grouping.**
> **The King uses beaters on three sides of the hunt.**
> **He lets the game go that runs before him.**
> **The capital's people need not be admonished.**
> **The Way is open.**

You are looking for people to be with and a social identity in which your relationship can find a place. Don't try to coerce or impress people. Always leave them a way out. This creates a true bond in which the people you contact are there because they want to be. Deep affinities have a chance to work. It shows people your sincerity. Acting like this opens the Way to real connections. *Direction*: Be open. Provide what is needed.

SIX ABOVE
> **A group without a head.**
> **The Way is closed.**

Either this is not the group for you and your Friend to join, or it is not the Friend to join with. There is no goal and no purpose. It is going nowhere fast. Leave now or face disaster. *Direction*: Take a deeper look. Strip away old ideas and be open to new ones.

9 Nurturing Small
HSIAO CH'U

小畜

Accumulate Small things to do the great; people helping one another; nurture, raise, support; develop through humility; dealings with the ghost world.

SETTING THE STAGE
Grouping needs a place to nurture things. Thus there comes the time of Nurturing the Small. Accept this. Do not fear. Nurturing the Small means at first you will have few.

OPENING THE FIELD
Nurture, CH'U: take care of, support, tolerate, encourage; help one another, overcome obstacles; tame, train; domesticate, raise, bring up; gather, collect, hoard, retain. The ideogram shows the fertile black soil of a river delta.

Small, HSIAO: little, flexible, adaptable; humility, what is common to all; adapt to whatever happens; make things Smaller, lessen, yin energy; the ghost world.

THE RESPONSE
Nurturing the Small will give you Success.
Shrouding clouds bring no rain yet.
We meet them at the Western Outskirts Altar.

Nurturing Small describes your relationship, or your part in it, in terms of confronting a great variety of things that may not seem to be related. The way to deal with it is to nurture and adapt to each thing in order to build something great. You are creating this relationship from scratch. Now is the time to help each other, to nurture strength in your relationship by taking care of one another. Take the long view. You don't have much to begin with. Accumulate affection and emotional power in Small ways. Deal with each thing in turn. Nurture the affection and the tolerance between you. Think of yourselves as raising children, growing crops or taming animals. The clouds that bring the rain are accumulating. Success and a deep connection are not far away.

SYMBOL, REFLECTION AND PRACTICE

Wind moves above Heaven. Nurturing the Small. An enduring force accumulates within as you gently understand each thing that occurs. You can turn discord into creative tension.

Reflection: A relationship is nothing in itself. It is the collection of all the individual things that people do with one another. You can develop a powerful and loving relationship with your Friend by dealing with the details of your lives, even though the variety and number may seem overwhelming. They will make or break your connection. Avoid trying to do too much at once. Content yourself with doing several Small things each day. Keep the end result in front of you. While celebrating your Small successes, accept what you still have to change. When things are not going as you would like, ask yourself, "What am I doing to contribute to this?" Then change what you do.

Practice: Spend time each day contemplating what you want with your Friend. Then imagine that the things you want are seeds made of light, harmony and love. Plant them in the fertile ground of your heart. Imagine tending them so that they grow beautifully. As the days pass, notice how beautifully these seeds have grown.

Transforming Lines

INITIAL NINE

> **Return to the origin of the Way.**
> **How could this be a mistake?**
> **The Way opens.**

You have been lost in a cloud of details, but now you see the Way clear once more. Don't hesitate to return to your Friend and the relationship. How could this be a mistake? The Way is open. *Direction*: Gently penetrate to the core. Turn conflict into creative tension. The situation is already changing.

Nine at Second

> **You return hauled along on a leash.**
> **The Way opens.**

You have been lost and confused. Now you are simply hauled back to your Friend and the relationship like an animal dragged on a leash. Consider yourself lucky. The Way is open to you. *Direction*: Stay within your family and dwelling. Gather energy for a decisive new move.

Nine at Third

> **The spokes of the cart are loosened.**
> **The husband and his consort roll their**
> **eyes in anger.**

A real family quarrel. Trying to do too much, the cart breaks down. You and your Friend are standing there rolling your eyes in indignation and nothing gets done. This is no Way to put your house in order. *Direction*: Find your own center. Take things in. Be open and provide what is needed.

Six at Fourth

> **There is a connection to the spirits.**
> **Bad blood leaves, alarms issue forth.**
> **This is not a mistake.**

You and your Friend can act with confidence now. The spirits are with you. Forget about old quarrels and resentments. Announce yourself and your new identity. This is not a mistake. Your purpose is united with those above. *Direction*: Take action. You are connected to a creative force.

NINE AT FIFTH

**There is a connection to the spirits through which
you are bound to others.
You can use your neighbor's affluence.**

You and your Friend are not alone. There is a spiritual connection that binds you to the people around you. Don't be afraid to make use of this connection. That's what it is for. Take hold of things. *Direction*: Be active. Find an idea that brings you together. Turn conflict into creative tension. The situation is already changing.

NINE ABOVE

**The rain has already come.
You already abide in honor, power and virtue.
Carry on!
Divination: adversity for the wife.
Be like the moon that is almost full.
If the Relating Person seeks to chastise others,
The Way will close.**

You and your Friend have achieved your goal. The rain has fallen to bless your relationship and together you live in honor and virtue. Don't worry, carry on. The Way of the wife faces danger that has its roots in the past. Don't try to put everything in order now. Don't discipline people. Don't set out on an expedition. These are the times the changes are made. Be like the moon that is almost full and the happiness you know now will endure. *Direction*: Wait for the right moment to act. Turn conflict into creative tension. The situation is already changing.

履 ☰ 10 Treading LÜ

Make your way a step at a time; trust in the outcome; conduct, support, sustain; good cheer, good luck.

SETTING THE STAGE

Beings are nurtured, then there are ways to follow that lead into life. Thus there comes the time of Treading. Accept this. Do not fear. Treading means not staying where you are.

OPENING THE FIELD

Tread, LÜ: walk, step; path, track, way; find your way, develop, cultivation; act, practice, accomplish; social cultivation; salary, position, means of subsistence; happiness, luck; the paths of the stars and planets. The ideogram shows feet walking.

THE RESPONSE

Treading on a Tiger's Tail.
It does not bite you. This will give you Success.

Treading describes your relationship, or your part in it, in terms of finding and making your Way together. The way to deal with it is to proceed step by step with trust in the outcome. The path is there. Walk it with good cheer and joy. You have to find your way, step by step, supporting and helping each other as you gain your livelihood. You are confronting a powerful force, walking in the tracks of the tiger, a powerful connection to creative spirit that can inspire and protect. If you are careful and perceptive, this great tiger will give you what you need. Speak to it carefully. Respect others. Meet the struggle cheerfully.

SYMBOL, REFLECTION AND PRACTICE

Sky above, the Mists below. Treading. Inner stimulation and

outer struggle create the steps of the path. Through this you find people to live and work with.

Reflection: You have the opportunity to participate in the wonders of increasing intimacy. Now is the time to cultivate your shared power. As you do, tread carefully, step by step. Give thought to what supports you both. Seek respect with each other, by respecting. Power is available to you within what you share. Until you make friends with this power, take care how you treat it. There is no need for it to frighten you. All the same, acting provocatively, disparagingly or unexpectedly could provoke unwanted responses. Act cheerfully with others and realize that the power you observe is your own.

Practice: As you sit quietly and still each day identify the powerful forces available inside and around you. Take each in turn and imagine yourself transformed into whatever it is. Experience this power, then wait as your experience stabilizes. Use the power you now experience to guide what you do during the day.

Transforming Lines

INITIAL NINE

Treading and going simply.
This is not a mistake.

Go your own way. Be simple and pure about your efforts. Move with your real desire. How could this be a mistake? *Direction:* Retire from conflicts. Stay in the family and the dwelling. Gather energy for a decisive new move.

NINE AT SECOND

Treading the Way, smoothing it, smoothing it.
Divination: the Way is open for people in shadow.

You are treading the Way, so be calm about everything. Your

relationship is fine. This is not the time to come out of hiding, however. Stay in the shade for now, hidden away. Your time will come. *Direction*: Disentangle yourself. Re-imagine the problem. Gather energy for a decisive new move.

Six at Third

> Someone squints and thinks they can see.
> Someone limps and thinks they can tread.
> Someone treads on the tiger's tail and gets bitten.
> The Way is closed.
> This is like a soldier acting as a Great Leader.

This is not the way to act in a real relationship. Give it up now. You are presuming on inadequate powers. Go on like this and the tiger will maul you. The only reason to act this way is if you had specific orders from your chief to sacrifice yourself. *Direction*: You confront a powerful and dangerous force.

Nine at Fourth

> Treading on the tiger's tail.
> Carefully, carefully present your petition.
> Bringing this to completion opens the Way.

You meet the great person, the source of power. Present your case clearly and persuasively. Don't be intimidated. The Way is open for your relationship. Your purpose is moving. *Direction*: Connect inner and outer life. Take things in. Be open to the new and provide what is needed.

Nine at Fifth

> Decisive treading and parting. Divination: adversity.

This next step in this relationship takes courage, because you must decisively separate yourselves from a dangerous past influence. Have no fear. Correcting the situation is definitely the right thing to do. *Direction*: Turn conflict into creative tension. The situation is already changing.

NINE ABOVE

> **As you look at your steps,**
> **the predecessors bless you.**
> **Their fertile recurrence opens the Way.**

If you look at the things you have been doing together, you will see that they connect with something that is bigger than your personal desires. Keep to this path, for the ancestors bless you. Learn to respect them, too, for it is their presence that opens the Way for the two of you. *Direction*: Come together joyously and express yourselves. Find supportive friends. Gather energy for a decisive new move.

泰 ䷊ 11 Pervading T'AI

Expand, communicate; harmony, abundance, flowering, connection.

SETTING THE STAGE

You tread the Way, then comes a time of Pervading and tranquillity. Accept this. Do not fear. Pervading means interpenetrating. Obstruction and Pervading reverses who you are classed with.

OPENING THE FIELD

Pervade, T'AI: peace, abundance, harmony, communion, love, prosperity, fertility; connection between Heaven and Earth; permeate, diffuse, smooth slippery; extreme, prodigious, extravagant. Mount T'ai (= pervading) was where the great sacrifices were made that connected Heaven and Earth. The ideogram shows someone standing in water, connected to the flow of life.

THE RESPONSE

Pervading. The Small goes, the Great comes.
The Way is open. This will give you Success.

Pervading describes your relationship, or your part in it, in terms of an influx of spirit that brings flowering, happiness and prosperity. The way to deal with it to spread this prosperity and joy by communicating in ever-widening circles. This is a time when Heaven and Earth come into conjunction and everything blossoms and flourishes. Your relationship is full of joy and spirit. What is Small and unimportant is leaving. What is great and significant is coming towards you.

This is a pivoting phase, where change can occur quickly and fundamentally. If you want to alter your relationship, apply yourself now.

SYMBOL, REFLECTION AND PRACTICE

Sky and Earth come together. Pervading. A creative force spreads from within. This is a time of abundance. If you let yourself be led, you can realize hidden potential.

Reflection: You are on the right track. You are doing what is needed to develop your relationship beautifully. Abundance is coming. Stay well connected to the Earth in your life. Connect to the Way and follow your intuition. You know what your Friend needs. It is inside you. As you connect clearly and strongly to yourself and to your heart, you also connect clearly to your Friend. Reach out for each other. You share great creative energy. Enjoy this and express it into the world together. Share it with others. Don't isolate yourselves from others. Discover who you are as a combined force. Sharing your joint creativity will bear great fruit. Stay true to yourselves as you respect the truth in others. Those actions that arise from truth will keep you in the Way.

Practice: Sit and imagine that a small version of you is sitting in your heart. Imagine, also, that you are sharing a heart-to-heart connection with your Friend. Encourage the softening, fuzzy, mellow energy coming from this connection to encompass you both. Let it perform its magic. Then progressively enfold others in the heart-field you are sharing.

Transforming Lines

INITIAL NINE
> **Pull up the twisted thatch-grass by the roots.**
> **Chastising opens the Way.**

It is time this relationship got off the ground. Take vigorous action to get out of this lowly place and find the people you really belong with. Be firm. Put things in order and set out. The Way is open. *Direction*: Make the effort. Turn conflict into creative tension. The situation is already changing.

Nine at Second

> **You are surrounded by a wasteland.**
> **Cross the channel. Don't put off leaving.**
> **Your partners will disappear.**
> **You acquire honor by moving to the center.**

You are surrounded by a wasteland, a tangled jungle where there is nothing of value to you. You have to act. Get out of this relationship. Cross the channel and move toward the center of things. The people you now identify with will disappear as you do this, but there is no other choice. Your integrity will be honored. *Direction*: Accept the hardship. In the end your light will shine. Release bound energy. The situation is already changing.

Nine at Third

> **Without the even, there is nothing uneven.**
> **Without going, there is no return.**
> **Divination: drudgery is not a mistake.**
> **Have no cares. You are connected to the spirit.**
> **You will find blessing in eating with others.**

You and your Friend are facing a difficult time. Remember, after a level road there is always a difficult climb. But if you don't let go of your joy, it will never come back to you. This difficulty is not a mistake. Don't worry, it has a real spiritual and emotional meaning. Eating together draws this blessing down. *Direction*: An important connection approaches. Something significant returns. Be open. Provide what is needed.

Six at Fourth
Fluttering, fluttering.
If you are not affluent, use what your
neighbor offers.
You do not need precautions. This is not a warning.
You are using your connection to the spirit.

You are afraid to leave the nest and make a commitment. Don't worry, come out and live in the great world. If you need help, then ask for it. There is nothing to feel bad about. You are using your basic connection to a Friend who is your spiritual kin. Act on your heart's desire. *Direction*: Fill yourself with invigorating strength. Be resolute. You are connected to a creative force.

Six at Fifth
The Great Ancestor converts the maiden.
This brings great satisfaction.
The Way to the Source is open.

This will be a great union that will have repercussions through the generations. It is an omen of future happiness that, in time, will gratify all your desires and realize all your aims. Take joy in this connection. The Way is fundamentally open. *Direction*: Wait for the right moment to act. Turn conflict into creative tension. The situation is already changing.

Six Above
The bulwarks fall back into the moat.
Don't use your legions now.
This message from fate has come from the capital.
Divination: distress and confusion.

The structure of your relationship is collapsing. Don't try to change things through acting aggressively. This has fate behind it. You may be confused but you are in the position to change your thinking. Take your time. Be of good cheer. You must collect the energy and insight to try again. *Direction:* Find a new central idea. Turn conflict into creative tension. The situation is already changing.

否 ☷ *12 Obstruction* PI

Stop!; obstacles, blocked communication; cut off, closed, failure; people of no use or worth to you.

SETTING THE STAGE

You cannot completely interpenetrate with others. Thus there comes the time of Obstruction. Accept this. Do not fear. Obstruction and Pervading reverse who you are classed with.

OPENING THE FIELD

Obstruction, PI: closed, stopped, blocked, bar the Way; unable to advance, failure, isolated, alienated; deny, refuse, disapprove; evil, wicked, perverse, unhappy, unfortunate. The ideogram suggests blocked communication.

THE RESPONSE

> **Obstruction and useless people.**
> **Divination: this is not advantageous for the**
> **Relating Person.**
> **The Great is going, the Small is coming.**

Obstruction describes your relationship, or your part in it, in terms of being blocked or interfered with. The way to deal with it is to stop pushing forward and accept the obstruction for now. You and/or your Friend are cut off, blocked by unfortunate occurrences and people who are of no value to you now. You will have to accept this. The main thing to do is to keep the faith and be sure of your affection. Almost anything else will encounter resistance and misfortune. You may be insulted and rejected. You simply cannot realize your plans directly. Adapt to the time and withdraw.

This is a pivoting phase, where change can occur quickly and fundamentally. If you want to alter your relationship, apply yourself now.

SYMBOL, REFLECTION AND PRACTICE

Sky and Earth do not come together. Obstruction. An outer struggle blocks inner creativity. In spite of everything you can gradually achieve your goal. You are advancing toward a marriage.

Reflection: You are individually or collectively entering a time of challenge. Communication is blocked by others who may seem petty, self-interested and concerned with things of little consequence. Yet they have the capacity to thwart what seems important to you. This is a time for owning your part in their behavior. Find where you are the same as they appear to be. Fully accept this in you. This will open you to accept the situation as it is and not fight it. Doing little or nothing for a while is the solution. These kinds of situations arise periodically and change with the passage of time. You may temporarily withdraw. Persisting through them without making radical or terminal decisions brings great rewards in the long run.

Practice: Whenever you notice anything obstructing you, take a few minutes to contemplate it. Allow yourself to experience your reactions as fully as possible, your feelings, thoughts and impulses. Whether the obstructions are inside or outside you, imagine yourself turning into them. Experience whatever this stimulates in you. The process will dissolve your side of the obstruction, perhaps gradually, provided you stay aware of the world around you. Then the Way will open again.

Transforming Lines

INITIAL SIX
> **Pull up the intertwisted thatch-grass by the roots.**
> **Divination: the Way opens. Success.**

It is time to pull back together. Take vigorous action to get out of this place and find the people you really belong with. Be firm. Put things in order and set out. The Way will open to you. You are assured of success. *Direction*: Disentangle yourself. Proceed step by step. Gather energy for a decisive new move.

SIX AT SECOND
> **Wrapped offerings.**
> **For Small People the Way is open.**
> **Great People are obstructed. Success.**

Accept that you are isolated even from your Friend. Make a hidden offering. You can succeed if you adapt to what crosses your path. Having a great idea will obstruct you. Stay true to yourself and the Way will open. *Direction*: Retreat from conflict. Find supportive friends. Gather energy for a decisive new move.

SIX AT THIRD
> **Wrapped offerings.**

Do nothing. Simply wait. Make inner preparations. The time is not right for action. Stop and examine yourself. *Direction*: Retire and be coupled with a creative force.

NINE AT FOURTH
> **There comes a mandate from on high.**
> **This is not a mistake.**
> **Cultivate this in radiant satisfaction.**

This is a connection made in Heaven and it is your job to try to make it real. In the middle of this terrible time, you experience what it is to be truly connected. Whatever happens, it is not a mistake to feel this way. Work at it. In the end it can bring you joy and satisfaction. In the end it can spread light to all. *Direction*: Let everything come into view. Strip away old ideas. Be open and provide what is needed.

NINE AT FIFTH

> **Relinquishing the obstruction.**
> **For the Great Person the Way opens.**
> **It disappears! it disappears!**
> **Attached to a grove of mulberry trees.**

If you are fighting the obstruction in the relationship, it is time to let go. When you truly feel the connection, the Way will open. The obstacles and troubles are disappearing. Imagine that you are in a quiet rural retreat. That is the place for you. It will correct the whole situation. *Direction*: You will emerge into the light. Re-imagine the situation. Gather energy for a decisive new move.

NINE ABOVE

> **Toppling obstructions.**
> **At first obstruction, then rejoicing.**

You think you are cut off from your Friend but suddenly the situation is turned on its head. What used to be an obstruction becomes a cause to rejoice. Thank Heavens the bad time is over! Let it all go. Why regret it? *Direction*: Gather people and resources for a great new project. Proceed step by step. Gather energy for a decisive new move.

同人 ☰ 13 *Concording People* T'UNG JEN

Bring people together, harmonize; share an idea or goal; welcome others, cooperate.

SETTING THE STAGE
You can't be completely obstructed. Thus there comes the time of Concording People. Accept this. Do not fear. Concording People means making new connections.

OPENING THE FIELD
Concord, T'UNG: unite, share, agree, bring together, harmonize; recognize common identity; compassion, union, concord, harmony; equalize, assemble, share; things held in common, the same time and place. The ideogram shows a cover and a mouth, suggesting silent understanding.
People, JEN: human beings, an individual and humanity as a whole. The ideogram shows a person kneeling in prayer.

THE RESPONSE
> Concording People in the countryside will
> give you Success.
> **It is advantageous to step into the Great River.**
> **Divination: advantageous for the Relating Person.**

Concording People describes your relationship, or your part in it, in terms of sharing and identifying with other people. The way to deal with it is to actively find ways to bring the people you are involved with together. To make your relationship work, you and your Friend must find a goal or an activity that you can share. This will harmonize the difficulties that usually separate you. Begin on the outskirts. Realize that you are facing the kind of task that can best be done together, like planting, harvesting or building. Embark on an ambitious new project. Step into the stream of life together with a shared goal. This sharing creates warmth and understanding.

SYMBOL, REFLECTION AND PRACTICE

Heaven unites with Fire. Concording People. Brightness and warmth spread outward through people's efforts to unite. A passionate connection. The primal powers come together.

Reflection: Act together, or find ways of coming together. The energy and times are right for this. Shared goals, particularly those that involve service, will help. Now is a time for moving into greater cooperation and intimacy with each other. Undertaking something new together is likely to succeed. Look for beauty and harmony and draw together to share it. Talk together. Concentrate on what you enjoy doing together and on where you are similar. You will strengthen and enhance what you have by doing so.

Practice: Sit quietly and still each day. Contemplate the qualities that you and your Friend have in common. Take each of these qualities and imagine yourself as your partner is with these qualities. Experience what this is like for you, avoid thinking. Celebrate the greater understanding of your Friend that this reveals.

Transforming Lines

INITIAL NINE

Concording people at the gate.
This is not a mistake.

You are poised on the threshold. Take the first step together. Announce your relationship. This is certainly not a mistake.

Direction: Retire from other engagements. You are coupled with a creative force.

SIX AT SECOND

> **Concording people in the ancestral hall.**
> **Distress and confusion.**

You and your Friend confront the ancestors, the models of behavior passed down through the generations. You are afraid you cannot live up to these standards. This is exactly the right feeling to have. As you think about it you will see the right way to act. *Direction*: Take action. You are coupled to a creative force.

NINE AT THIRD

> **Hiding arms in the thickets and ascending**
> **your high mound.**
> **For three years' time you won't rise up.**

You have fallen victim to feelings of resentment. You have been treated badly and you withdraw from your Friend. Be careful. Are you sure you want to act like this? It will keep you isolated for quite a long time. *Direction*: Disentangle yourself. Proceed step by step. Gather energy for a decisive new move.

NINE AT FOURTH

> **Ride your ramparts.**
> **Nothing can control or attack you.**
> **The Way is open.**

You and your Friend are deeply connected and very clear about your relationship. Trust it. Stay within it. Let it give you the courage to go on. Nothing can stop you. The Way is open. *Direction*: Stay in your family and dwelling. Gather energy for a decisive new move.

NINE AT FIFTH
> **Concording people first cry out and sob
> and then they laugh.
> The Great Leaders control their mutual meeting.**

The Way to a loving relationship is not easy. There is often pain, loneliness and separation involved when two people want to come together. But when you work your way through the tears, the joy is there. As long as your hearts are firm, everything you encounter will conspire to help you. "Sweet as the fragrance of orchids, it shatters the strength of iron." *Direction*: Spread warmth and awareness. Don't be afraid to act alone. You are connected to a creative force.

NINE ABOVE
> **Concording People at the Outskirts Altar.
> Without a cause for sorrow.**

You and your Friend don't have a purpose yet. You can find it by peeling away the dead skin. Give it a try. You won't have any cause to regret it. *Direction*: Take off the skin. Take action. You are coupled to a creative force.

14 Possessing the Great TA YU

大有 ☰

A great idea; great power to realize things; organization, concentration; wealth, abundance, possessions; great results, great achievements; share your wealth.

SETTING THE STAGE

Associating with concording people means that others will be sincerely converted to your idea. Thus comes the time of Possessing the Great. Accept this. Do not fear. Possessing the Great gathers crowds around you.

OPENING THE FIELD

Possess, YU: to be, to exist; have, own, possessions, goods; dispose of, arise, occur; events. The ideogram suggests sharing with the spirits and with other people.
Great, TA: big, noble, important; able to protect others; orient your will to a self imposed goal; yang energy.

THE RESPONSE
Possessing the Great will give you Fundamental Success.

Possessing the Great describes your relationship, or your part in it, in terms of obtaining abundance and prosperity through the development of a unifying idea. The way to deal with it is to concentrate your energies in one place and share the fruits of your efforts. You and your Friend can acquire real abundance and prosperity, emotional and material, by working together to develop a central idea. Concentrate your energy and focus on a single goal. Be generous with each other and with other people.

By continually circulating the wealth you obtain, your relationship becomes a deep and continuing source of success and excellence. Make a great offering together.

SYMBOL, REFLECTION AND PRACTICE

Fire above Sky. Possessing the Great. Force concentrates within, spreading brightness and warmth. This is a time of great abundance. You can act clearly and decisively to part with the old.

Reflection: Commit yourselves to what is important to you. Concentrate on what you want to have in your lives together— love, beauty, fun, productivity. As you do this, you will strengthen those qualities. Let go of anger, fear, and sadness. Avoid holding grudges. Deliberately do as many loving things as possible. Release yourself from what is not loving. Think loving thoughts. Feel love. Surround yourself with beauty. Individually or jointly you have something. Take advantage of what you have together to plan. Decide how you will act and follow through. Act with confidence. It is all right to be noticed. Share what you have through definite action. Such sharing can add new excitement, depth and breadth to your relationship.

Practice: Sit quietly and still for a few minutes each day. Imagine that small replicas of you and your Friend have moved into your heart or into the middle of your head, whichever seems the easiest. Locate yourself in one of these centers, then include the other in your awareness. As your head and heart come together, love and wisdom will surround you both. Open yourself to spiritual energy by concentrating on the clearest, lightest, sweetest or most refined aspects of your experience. Open yourself to life's Heavenly origins.

Transforming Lines

Initial Nine

Without mingling harm.
This is not a mistake.
The drudgery involved is also not a mistake.

There is nothing harmful in your relationship. You are not making a mistake in feeling the way you do. There is a lot of hard work involved. This drudgery isn't a mistake either. *Direction*: You can connect to the spirits and establish something enduring. Be resolute. You are connected to a creative force.

Nine at Second

Use a Great Chariot to carry it.
Have a direction to go. This is not a mistake.

Your relationship has to have a vehicle, an inspiring idea that can carry your feelings. Make a plan. Dedicate yourself to it. You will not be making a mistake. *Direction*: Spread warmth and awareness. Don't be afraid to act alone. You are coupled with a creative force.

Nine at Third

A prince makes a sacrifice to the Son of Heaven.
Small People cannot control it.

This is the moment of truth. Concentrate everything you feel for your friend and offer it to the highest principle you know. Do not let other people control your ideas. This will create a firm and lasting connection. *Direction*: Turn conflict into creative tension. The situation is already changing.

NINE AT FOURTH

> **Do not seek dominance.**
> **This is not a mistake.**

Don't try to be the boss. The time is wrong for that. Let your Friend shine. Bring out other people's qualities. Be very clear about this. You will not be making a mistake. *Direction*: Gather energy for a great undertaking. You can realize hidden potential. The situation is already changing.

SIX AT FIFTH

> **You really have a connection to the spirits!**
> **If you mingle with others, you will impress them.**

You have made the connection and everyone is going to be impressed. Act with complete confidence. Stay true to your purpose and stay true to your Friend. Be versatile. With spirit like this you can deal with anything. *Direction*: You are in contact with a creative force.

NINE ABOVE

> **Heaven shields its birth.**
> **The Way is open.**
> **There is nothing for which this will not**
> **be advantageous.**

Heaven protects you, your Friend and the birth of your relationship. The Way is open to you. In the long run, this will benefit everyone. *Direction*: Invigorate your sense of purpose. Be resolute. You are connected to a creative force.

謙 ☷ 15 *Humbling* CH'IEN

Balance, adjust, cut through pride and complications; stay close to fundamentals; think of yourself and your desires in a modest way; accept unconscious processes.

SETTING THE STAGE

Possessing the Great does not allow you to fill things to overflowing. Thus there comes the time of Humbling. Accept this. Do not fear. Humbling means becoming agile. Humbling activates unconscious creative powers.

OPENING THE FIELD

Humble, CH'IEN: think and speak of yourself in a modest way; polite, simple, respectful; cut through pride and complication; balance and adjust, harmonize; yielding, compliant, reverent. The ideogram suggests keeping words connected to facts.

THE RESPONSE

Humbling will give you Success.
For the Relating Person what is desired will be
brought to completion.

Humbling describes your relationship, or your part in it, in terms of cutting through pride and complication. The way to deal with it is to keep your words and thoughts simple and connected to fundamental things. You and your Friend are working to perfect a real connection. Don't let your pride or your inner complications get in the way. Stay simple and connected to the facts. Think of yourself in a modest, humble way. Keep your words clear and sincere. This helps you cut through the snares of the ego. If you voluntarily take the lower position, you will release transformative energy and assure yourself of success. Use the oracle to stay in touch with the Way and you will be able to bring your desires to completion. You will not bring things to an end, but open new beginnings. Cutting through pride and the need to dominate brings a great power of realization. Be clear about this, then act directly.

SYMBOL, REFLECTION AND PRACTICE
Mountain in the middle of Earth. Humbling. The inner sense of limits sustains generous and loving behavior. You and your Friend can be freed from tension and compulsion.

Reflection: This is a time for willingly making way for others. Staying humble is, however, different from adopting a pretended posture of deference. Keeping what is important at the center of your activities will help you find balance inside yourself and with others. Wonderful learning is available now. Being fully with someone at times means letting go of trying to be right or the most important one. Practice saying "Yes" first, instead of, "No". You have the chance to deepen and strengthen your connections with each other. What is most important to you, continuing with your Friend, or winning the game? You might decide to go along with his or her wishes, even though you would normally not do so.

Practice: Sit for a few minutes in silence. Allow any aspect of your relationship to occur to you. Affirm, "I am available" to anything that comes into your awareness. Keep doing it until you experience full acceptance of whatever it is. Do something simple to express this acceptance with your Friend.

Transforming Lines

INITIAL SIX
The Relating Person humbling again and again.
Step into the Great River. The Way is open.

Work hard at making this relationship work. Keep your pride out of the way. Think everything through twice, then take the big step. The Way is open to you and your Friend. *Direction*: Accept difficulties. Release bound energy. The situation is already changing.

SIX AT SECOND

Humbling calling out.
Divination: the Way is open.

The inner work you are doing calls out to your Friend like the cry birds use to recognize each other. Don't hesitate. The Way opens for you both. *Direction*: Make the effort. Let yourself be led. You can realize hidden potential. The situation is already changing.

NINE AT THIRD

The Relating Person toils humbly.
You bring what you desire to completion.
The Way is open.

You humbly work at this relationship, following its connection to the Way. Carry on. You don't need to advertise. What you desire will simply appear. *Direction*: Be open. Provide what is needed.

SIX AT FOURTH

Demonstrating humbling.
There is nothing for which this will not
be advantageous.

Let your actions show what humbling really is. If you can do this, everything in your relationship will benefit. Don't be attached to your ideas and do not get involved in arguments. *Direction*: Careful attention to the Small. Don't be afraid to act alone. You are connected to a creative force.

Six at Fifth

> **If you are not affluent, you may use your**
> **neighbor's wealth.**
> **It is advantageous to vigorously attack what**
> **you have to do.**
> **There is nothing for which this will not**
> **be advantageous.**

You and your Friend are acting together. The relationship works. It is time to expand. Take what you need from the people who offer. Work together. Do not be timid. Attack your problems aggressively. Everything will benefit from this behavior. *Direction:* Re-imagine the situation. Gather energy for a decisive new move.

Six Above

> **Humbling calling out.**
> **It is advantageous to move your legions**
> **and chastise the capital city.**

The inner power of your relationship calls out to you. It is time to expand. Focus your energies on a major plan, marshal your forces and attack. You can set right your place in the social world and eliminate negativity. *Direction:* Articulate past experiences. Release bound energy. The situation is already changing.

豫 ䷏ 16 *Providing For* YÜ

**Prepare, collect what you need to meet the future;
spontaneous, direct response, enthusiastic; enjoy,
take pleasure.**

SETTING THE STAGE

Possessing the Great and the ability to be humble will provide for
any situation. Thus there must come the time of Providing For.
Accept this. Do not fear. Providing For means you become gentle
and alert.

OPENING THE FIELD

Provide For, YÜ: take precautions, arrange for, make ready;
happy, content, prepared for; joyous, pleasure, delight; spontaneous response, enthusiasm, carried away. The ideogram suggests
that being prepared lets you respond spontaneously.

THE RESPONSE

**Providing For.
It is advantageous to install helpers and
move the legions.**

Providing For describes your relationship, or your part in it, in
terms of gathering what is needed to meet and enjoy what the
future brings. You can deal with it by accumulating the strength
and insight to respond spontaneously and fully when the time
comes to act. By developing this inner strength, both together and
alone, you can enjoy your love freely and openly. You can respond
together spontaneously when the impulse comes. You can take
pleasure in each other. Think things through. Understand what
you might be up against. Look at your problems. Involve other
people, so that you can mobilize powerful help when necessary. If

you prepare yourself this way, your accumulated energy will bound out of the Earth when the heart opens and the call comes.

SYMBOL, REFLECTION AND PRACTICE

Thunder bounds from Earth. Providing For. Through inner toil you accumulate the strength to respond joyously. You will be able to re-imagine a difficult situation.

Reflection: Good times provide opportunities both for enjoyment and for building the future. Do both with each other now. Delight in what you have together and take stock. Find what strengthens you both and build on it together. Concentrate on building a store of loving energy. All efforts to do this will benefit you both. Offer many small, everyday expressions of love and appreciation. These help form the foundations of great partnerships. Then in times of stress or need, loving resources will be abundant and available. Cultivate receptivity to love. Love comes from union, not a one-way flow. Love forms a wonderful backdrop to dealing with difficulties, too. Take advantage of your current opportunity. You will bless the day that you did.

Practice: Sit for a few minutes each day. Imagine yourself filling with loving, harmonious and brilliant energy. With each in-breath, it flows into you. Each out-breath anchors this life energy securely inside you, allowing you to release unhelpful energies. Affirm that the beautiful energy is precisely what you need for what is coming.

Transforming Lines

INITIAL SIX

Calling for provision.
The Way closes.

You are trying to get your Friend to take care of you. It doesn't work like that. You have to sort this one out yourself. If you keep calling for help you will exhaust the relationship. *Direction*: A fertile shock! Re-imagine the situation. Gather energy for a decisive new move.

Six at Second
> **The limits are turning to stone.**
> **Don't even complete the day.**
> **Divination: the Way opens.**

The rules in this relationship are so rigid they are turning you both to stone. Don't wait. Let go of them now. The Way is open to you. Correct yourself and release the bound energy. *Direction*: Release bound energy.

Six at Third
> **Skeptical providing for brings cause for sorrow.**
> **Holding back brings cause for sorrow.**

Don't be skeptical about this relationship and don't hold back. This is real. Doubting and equivocating will only bring you sorrows. Provide what is needed, simply and directly. You won't be sorry about that. *Direction*: Be very careful of details. Don't be afraid to act alone. You are connected to a creative force.

Nine at Fourth
> **Previous provision.**
> **Great acquisitions.**
> **Do not doubt.**
> **You join your Friends as a hair clasp gathers in the hair.**

This is a match made in Heaven. Have no doubts. You join together like a sweet embrace. Together your purpose can move mountains. *Direction*: Be open and provide what is needed.

Six at Fifth

> **Divination: there is affliction.**
> **Persevere, you will not die.**

This is a hard time—sickness, hostility, isolation, disorder, pain. But don't give up on your relationship. It and you will certainly survive. *Direction*: Gather resources for a great new project. Proceed step by step. Gather energy for a decisive new move.

Six Above

> **Dark providing.**
> **Your accomplishments are collapsing.**
> **This is not your mistake.**

You are groping in the dark. You don't really know what this relationship needs, so your real accomplishments are falling apart. This isn't your fault, but why let it go on any longer. Admit your ignorance, climb out of the cave and meet your Friend in the light of day. *Direction*: Emerge into the light. Re-imagine the situation. Gather energy for a decisive new move.

隨 ䷐ *17 Following* SUI

Move with the flow, strong, natural attraction; inevitable, natural, correct; influence, guidance.

SETTING THE STAGE

Providing for people's needs will necessarily create following. Thus there comes the time of Following. Accept this. Do not fear. Following does away with all the old sorrows.

OPENING THE FIELD

Follow, SUI: yield to a strong attraction; come in sequence; influence, guidance; conform to, in the style of, follow a Way, school or religion; move in the same direction; natural, correct, inevitable. The ideogram shows three footsteps, one after the other.

THE RESPONSE

**Following will give you Fundamental Success
and an Advantageous Divination.
This is not a mistake.**

Following describes your relationship, or your part in it, in terms of being drawn forward by a powerful and natural influence. You can deal with it by yielding to the flow of events. These feelings are natural, correct and an inevitable part of your life. Yield to what is in front of you. Follow the path of least resistance. Be guided by the way things are moving. You have been drawn into an interconnected chain of events that will change your life. This relationship will bring you fundamental success, profit and insight. The call has come. Follow it. Don't try to take the lead. Give in to the power of the connection.

SYMBOL, REFLECTION AND PRACTICE

Thunder in the middle of the Mists. Following. Outer stimulation rouses new energy within. You can gradually realize all your desires.

Reflection: Follow the current flow of events. The tree is present in the seed. Your future relationship is present in the loving connection you now have. Underlying the current situation there is a basic change going on. To ensure a rich and deep relationship, you need to allow this deep evolution to take place as well. Holding onto the way you did things in the past will block this growth. Let go and concentrate on loving in the present. You don't need to make anything happen. Allow changes to arise within yourselves, then express them naturally.

Practice: Each day, do at least three things, no matter how small, that express directly what you are experiencing at the time. If feeling loving, reach out and touch; if enjoying beauty, say something about it or just sigh; if irritated, grumble a little. Notice how this creates openness and how this makes following easier.

Transforming Lines

INITIAL NINE

> **If you have an office, deny it.**
> **Divination: the Way is open.**
> **Issue forth from the gate and mingle with others.**
> **There will be achievements.**

Leave your old life behind. This relationship will transform you. Walk out of your old thoughts and mix with new people. This will definitely produce new achievements. The Way has opened to you. *Direction*: Gather resources for a great new project. Re-imagine the situation. Gather energy for a decisive new move.

SIX AT SECOND

> Tied to the Small Son,
> You let the Respectable Husband go.

This relationship is a mistake. You have picked the wrong person to follow. You will end up alone, without anyone to trust. All you can do is adapt to whatever crosses your path. *Direction:* Be cheerful. Express yourself. Find supportive friends. Gather energy for a decisive new move.

SIX AT THIRD

> Tied to the Respectable Husband,
> You let the Small Son go.
> Through following, you seek and acquire
> what you desire.
> Divination: advantageous for a residence.

You have made the right choice. You are following the right person. You will get everything you desire from this relationship. Staying right where you are brings you profit and insight. *Direction:* Change the way you present yourself. It will couple you with a creative force.

NINE AT FOURTH

> Following in order to catch something.
> Divination: the Way closes.
> If you connect to the spirits and locate yourself
> in the Way,
> Your understanding will be brightened.
> How could that be a mistake?

You are trying to trap your love. You have turned following into a kind of hunt. This will not work. However, you can change things easily if you want to. Connect with the spirit rather than your ego, and put yourself in the Way. Then things will come of themselves. You will understand what it is to follow rather than pursue. Your sense of purpose is leading you astray. *Direction:* This is an important new beginning. Strip away old ideas. Be open to the new. Provide what is needed.

NINE AT FIFTH

> **A connection to the spirit that leads to excellence.**
> **The Way opens.**

You have made the connection. This relationship will work. It will lead you onto real achievements. Have no doubts. Follow it. The Way is open to you. *Direction:* Stir things up and act. Gather energy for a decisive new move.

SIX ABOVE

> **Grappled and tied,**
> **The adherents are held fast.**
> **The King makes sacrifice and receives blessings**
> **on the Western Mountain.**

You are firmly attached to the person you follow. Other people are held fast through your devotion. You are enshrined in the hall of ancestors. You help in the flow of blessings. *Direction:* Stay disentangled. Re-imagine the situation. Gather energy for a decisive new move.

蠱 ䷑ 18 Corruption/ Renovating KU

Perversion, decay, negative effects of the past, of parents on children; black, sexual magic; renew, renovate, find a new beginning.

SETTING THE STAGE

Rejoicing and following means there will be things to attend to. Thus there comes the time of Corruption and Renovating. Accept this. Do not fear. Corruption means attending to things and doing business. Corruption and Renovation bring stability.

OPENING THE FIELD

Corrupt, KU: rotten, poisonous, defiled; intestinal worms, venomous insects; perversion, evil effects of parents and the past; black magic; seduce, pervert, flatter, put under a spell; disorder, error; engage in business. The ideogram shows poisonous insects in a jar that is used for black magic.

THE RESPONSE

> **Corruption and Renovating will give you**
> **Fundamental Success.**
> **It is advantageous to step into the Great River.**
> **Before seedburst three days, after seedburst three days.**

Corruption describes your relationship, or your part in it, in terms of putrefaction, dark magic and the deeds done by parents and ancestors that may be harming their children. The way to deal with it is get to the source of this within yourselves so that a new beginning can be found. Your relationship is suffering from the effects of the parental past. You have to deal with this hidden influence if you want to continue. Seek out the source of this corruption within yourselves and change it. Step into the stream of life with this purpose. Prepare the change carefully. Watch over its beginning and guide its growth. Rouse the hidden potential of the love and connection between you. You can create a brand new flowering. There is plenty to do. The spirit is truly moving in your relationship.

SYMBOL, REFLECTION AND PRACTICE

Wind below Mountain. Corruption. Outer limits turn growth back on itself and corrupt it. Through renovating, you can realize your hidden potential.

Reflection: Take the opportunity to explore harmful remnants from your pasts, your parents and figures of authority. Doing this can free the core of what you share from accumulated poisons. Take responsibility for what you each contribute to your current situation. Support and encourage each other as you go about this work. Deep change can come from this and open the Way for a much greater love and creativity. Remind yourselves that the primal urge for complete openness is driving you to face these things. Look back to your family origins for the sources of what you now experience. Heal this past by changing yourself. Sit quietly and imagine that Heavenly energy is filling you. It flows into and through you, releasing, cleansing, healing and carrying out everything that is unhelpful. In fantasy, repeat the relevant past events several times. With each repetition, imagine change, to make your fantasy of the events closer to how you needed and/or wanted your past to have been. Briefly get up and move around physically, after each time. Keep repeating these steps until you can think back and experience resolution, release and healing. Remember to keep your overall concentration on the outcomes you both want.

Practice: Sit quietly and imagine that Heavenly energy is filling you. It flows into and through you, releasing, cleansing, healing and carrying out everything that is unhelpful. Finish when you are filled with divine energy and all else has gone. Do something each day to express your fullness into the physical world.

Transforming Lines

INITIAL SIX
Managing the Father's corruption.
The child corrects the faults of the predecessors.
Completing this adversity opens the Way.

If your relationship is to survive you must deal with the corruption of authority. This is danger with roots in the past that haunts you both. If you manage this, the Way will open. Take on the responsibility like a son or daughter who redeems the ancestors and go through it to the end. *Direction:* Concentrate. Focus. Be active. If you let yourself be led, you can realize hidden potential. The situation is already changing.

NINE AT SECOND
Managing the Mother's corruption.
This does not allow a divination.

You must deal with the corruption of nourishment and caring within your relationship. Asking the oracle won't help you. You must simply put yourself in the middle of the situation and try to find the Way. Then you will be able to see the obstruction. *Direction:* Find and articulate the obstacles. Release bound energy. The situation is already changing.

NINE AT THIRD
Managing the Father's corruption.
Small sorrows.
Being without the Great is a mistake.

You must deal with the corruption of authority within your relationship. There will be regrets that you co-operated with it. The two of you must have a strong central purpose to come through.

Direction: There is something hidden that will unfold in this situation. Be open and provide what is needed.

Six at Fourth
Enriching the father's corruption.
Going on like this will bring distress and confusion.

You are colluding with the corruption of authority that is destroying your relationship. If you go on like this you will end up both lonely and confused. *Direction:* Transform your awareness. Be resolute. You are connected with a creative force.

Six at Fifth
Managing the Father's corruption.
Use praise to accomplish the task.

You must deal with the corruption of authority within your relationship. Don't attack directly. Use praise to accomplish the task. You will disarm your opponent and reclaim your own power. In the process you will find out what your purpose really is. *Direction:* Gently penetrate to the core of the problem. Turn conflict into creative tension. The situation is already changing.

Nine Above
Don't involve yourself in the affairs of
Kings and Servants.
Honoring what is highest is your affair.

You and your Friend should keep clear of business and politics. You have another job, finding and honoring what is truly noble in the human spirit. This describes people who work in the darkness to prepare an awakening. *Direction:* Make the effort. If you let yourself be led, you can realize hidden potential. The situation is already changing.

臨 ䷒ *19 Nearing* LIN

Arrival of the new; approach of something powerful and meaningful; welcome, draw nearer and closer.

Setting the Stage
These are affairs that allow the Great to approach. Thus there comes the time of nearing. Accept this. Do not fear. Nearing means the Great. Nearing and Viewing are both proper now. Sometimes you will associate with people, sometimes you must seek them out.

Opening the Field
Nearing, LIN: a beneficent spirit or an honored person approaches to confer favor and blessing; look at with love, care and sympathy; arrive, make contact, point of arrival; be honored with a visit, be commanded to come nearer.

The Response
> **Nearing will give you Fundamental Success and an advantageous divination.**
> **Ending this in the eighth moon-month closes the Way.**

Approaching describes your relationship, or your part in it, in terms of something great that is approaching you. The way to deal with it is to simply welcome this arrival, without immediately expecting to get what you want. Something is approaching that will confer great blessing and joy. This is the point of contact, the arrival of the new, and it will completely change your relationship. Welcome the approach. This contact can open up a whole new time. It brings fundamental success, profit and insight. Don't rush to completion. A premature harvest would close the Way.

Symbol, Reflection and Practice

Earth above Mists. Nearing. Inner cheer and a willingness to serve invite Nearing. There will be a fundamental return of the spirit.

Reflection: Something wonderful is approaching. A deep force is close, a force on which you will be able to call. Look for it within yourselves and in each other. Attract it by cultivating openness to and caring for your Friend. Act lovingly and honestly with each other. Keeping things light and clear will make you more attractive to whatever is coming. If seeking a Friend, practice patience and realize that you are about to be offered a great gift. Make yourself open and appealing. Avoid expecting too much and acting as if small hints indicate big commitments. More time is required, so your persistence is necessary.

Practice: Begin by being still for a few minutes. Notice your contact with what is physically underneath you. After a short time, imagine a small replica of you has centered itself in your heart. Welcome everything you notice yourself experiencing; welcome without expectation. Whatever it is may grow into something more, it may disappear, or it may return. Simply smile and be available, whatever happens.

Transforming Lines

Initial Nine

Conjunction nearing.
Divination: the Way is open.

The person approaching belongs with you like parts of a previously separated whole. This is a marriage made in Heaven. It will stimulate and inspire you. Have no doubts. The Way is open. *Direction*: Organize your forces. This is the return of something important. Be open. Provide what is needed.

NINE AT SECOND

> Conjunction nearing. The Way is open.
> There is nothing for which this will not
> be advantageous.

The person approaching belongs with you like parts of a previously separated whole. This is a marriage made in Heaven. It will stimulate and inspire you. There is nothing that will not benefit from this connection. The good consequences have hardly begun. *Direction:* This is the return of something important. Be open. Provide what is needed.

SIX AT THIRD

> Sweetly nearing,
> With no advantageous direction.
> If you are already grieving, there will be no mistake.

What is approaching may look sweet but no good can come of it. This person is simply not right for you. Painful though it may be, if you have already realized it you won't make mistakes. *Direction:* This change begins a flourishing new time. Turn conflict into creative tension. The situation is already changing.

SIX AT FOURTH

> Culmination nearing.
> This is not a mistake.

This is the climax of your relationship. Don't hold back. Give yourself fully. This is not a mistake. *Direction:* Turn conflict into creative tension. The situation is already changing.

SIX AT FIFTH

> Knowledge nearing
> The Great Leader sacrifices at the Earth Altar.
> The Way is open.

Your relationship has a special quality, the knowledge a great leader uses to help and change people. Don't ignore this part of your connection with your Friend. This can change the way you see yourself and your life. *Direction:* Articulate this. Find your voice. Take things in. Provide what is needed.

SIX ABOVE

> **Generosity and wealth nearing.**
> **The Way opens.**
> **This is not a mistake.**

Generosity, wealth and the power of enjoyment enter your life through your relationship. Be generous with what you acquire. Hold onto your sense of inner purpose. Your desires will be satisfied. *Direction:* Decrease present involvement to make new energy available. Something important returns. Provide what is needed.

觀 ☰☰ *20 Viewing* KUAN

**Let everything come into view, examine, contemplate,
divine the meaning.**

SETTING THE STAGE
Through being Great you are allowed to divine and offer sacrifice. Thus there comes the time of Viewing. Accept this. Do not fear. Nearing and Viewing are both proper now. Sometimes you will associate with people, sometimes you must seek them out.

OPENING THE FIELD
View, KUAN: contemplate, look at from a distance, examine, judge, conjecture; let everything emerge into view; divine the meaning; instruct, inform, make known; a Taoist monastery, tower, observatory. The ideogram suggests a bird's eye view and watching for bird signs.

THE RESPONSE
**Viewing, the ablutions then the libation.
The connection to spirit will come like a presence.**

Viewing describes your relationship, or your part in it, in terms of the need to look at everything without acting. The way to deal with it is to let everything emerge into view so you can divine its significance. There is something out of key going on and you must find out what it is. Let go of your need to control and let everything emerge. Particularly look at things that you usually don't want to see. Then you will be able to divine the meaning and find the right perspective. Have confidence. Looking into things, no matter how painful, will bring you the insight you need to go on. This is like a religious ceremony where you make preparations to pour out the wine that calls the spirit.

SYMBOL, REFLECTION AND PRACTICE

Wind moves above Earth. Viewing. Images of distant things and actions come into view on the inner field. Strip away your outmoded thoughts and memories.

Reflection: Step back and look at your relationship from a distance. Take the time to do this alone or together. Actively consider all aspects, particularly the most challenging. Always remember that the challenges and the answers lie primarily within you. This important review is prompted from deep within each of you, and the strength and tenacity you need to do it is available. So keep going. Great and timely change is here. You will need to step out of your habitual ways of doing things to do this properly. Stay aware of and avoid censoring what you notice. Everything is important. Remember to pay attention to what is working well. Problems lose much of their power when you do this.

Practice: Sit still for a few minutes each day. Pay attention to the point between your eyebrows by internally looking at, listening to, or feeling that spot. It is an opening to the combined influence and beauty of Heaven and Earth. Consider the way you relate to your Friend, while relating to this point. Allow new perspectives, themes and orientations to reveal themselves.

Transforming Lines

INITIAL SIX

Young viewing.
For Small People this is not a mistake.
A Relating Person sees distress and confusion.

You are looking at your Friend and your relationship like a child. That is fine if you want to live like a child, dependent and at the mercy of other people's feelings. If you want a real relationship, however, this leads to distress and confusion. *Direction*: Increase your efforts. Strip away old ideas. Be open and provide what is needed.

SIX AT SECOND
Viewing through a patterned screen.
Advantageous if the woman makes the Divination.

You are spying on your Friend, trying to find out his or her secrets. This is fine if you want to act like a traditional powerless person. It is not so good if you want to claim your own inner power. Empower the woman to ask the questions. *Direction*: Clear away obstacles to understanding. Take things in. Be open and provide what is needed.

SIX AT THIRD
Viewing my birth, advance or withdraw?

This is a transition. You have to decide whether to go on with this relationship or to pull back. Look at the things you do together, what you give birth to, what the relationship creates in you. Use that to answer your question. *Direction*: Proceed step by step. Gather energy for a decisive new move.

SIX AT FOURTH
Viewing the shining of the city.
It is advantageous to be a guest
When the King entertains the Ancestors.

Your relationship will bring you power and wealth. The city is spread out before you. Remember, however, you are a guest. Be careful and polite. This is a long-term experience. *Direction*: Communication may be obstructed. Proceed step by step. Gather energy for a decisive new move.

NINE AT FIFTH

Viewing our birth.
The Relating Person makes no mistake.

Look deeply at this connection and your relation to it. Look at the things you do together, what you give birth to, what the relationship creates in you. Then commit yourself. If you measure your desires against the ideal of the Relating Person, you won't make any mistakes. *Direction:* Strip away old ideas. Provide what is needed.

NINE ABOVE

Viewing its birth.
The Relating Person makes no mistake.

Look deeply at this connection and your relation to it. Look at where and how it started and the effect it has had on your life and the life of your Friend. Then commit yourself. If you measure it against the ideal of the Relating Person, you won't make any mistakes. *Direction:* Change who you associate with. Strip away old ideas. Be open and provide what is needed.

噬
嗑 ☲ *21 Gnaw and Bite Through* SHIH HO

Confront the problem, bite through the obstacle, tenacious, determined, enduring.

SETTING THE STAGE
When you are allowed to divine and make sacrifices, you can create a place to unite. Thus there comes the time of Gnawing and Biting Through obstacles. Accept this. Do not fear. Gnawing and Biting Through means uniting. Gnawing and Biting Through means eating your way through any problems.

OPENING THE FIELD
Gnaw and Bite Through: Confront the problem, bite through the obstacle, tenacious, determined, enduring.

Gnaw, SHIH HO: bite, chew, nibble away; arrive at the truth, attain the goal, remove what is extraneous and reveal what is necessary. The ideogram suggests finding truth through divination.

Bite Through: unite, bring together; close the jaws, crush, chew; destroy an obstacle. The ideogram shows things coming together.

THE RESPONSE
Gnawing and Biting Through will give you success.
It is advantageous to use rules and take measures.

Gnawing and Biting Through describes your relationship, or your part in it, in terms of an obstacle dividing you that will not simply go away by itself. The way to deal with it is to gnaw away the unnecessary and bite through the core of the problem. You must take determined, decisive action. Don't give up. If you keep at it, you will get down to the essentials and bite through the resistance. This is a time for legal actions, punishments and warnings to criminals. Determination and clarity are absolutely essential. You have thought about it long enough. Now get to work!

SYMBOL, REFLECTION AND PRACTICE

Thunder and Lightning. Gnawing and Biting Through. An inner force bites through outer obstacles. You can re-imagine this difficult situation.

Reflection: Standing your ground and doing what is right is important now, even with those you love. Waiting longer will not work. Do what is necessary. Respect from others usually follows right action, often when taken in the face of stiff opposition. Giving in usually loses respect. Go inside and deal internally with your own part in what is going on. Remember that your Friend is reflecting you back to yourself. This is a great opportunity for personal growth and for strengthening your relationship. Be determined and persistent. The rewards for success are great. Lovers and Friends sometimes need to set limits with each other. If something seems right to you, stand your ground.

Practice: Sit and imagine that you have turned into your Friend. You take on, sound like and look like every aspect of him or her. Let this process stimulate your own awareness of your part in what is not working for either or both of you. Find where you need to take a stand with yourself through what you do. Commit to the action and follow through. Notice what changes in your relationship with your Friend.

Transforming Lines

INITIAL NINE
> Locked in a wooden stock, your feet disappear.
> This is not a mistake.

You are the prisoner this time. Trying to control the relationship, you have been locked up and cut off from your Friend. Don't worry. This is for your own good. It is the right thing to do now. It will make you think. *Direction*: You will emerge into the light and be recognized. Re-imagine the situation. Gather your energy for an impressive new move.

SIX AT SECOND

> **Gnawing through flesh, your nose disappears.**
> **This is not a mistake.**

Enthusiastically biting through obstacles between you and your Friend, you go a little overboard. Don't worry. Keep it up. This is not a mistake. You are on the right track. *Direction*: Turn conflict into creative tension. The situation is already changing.

SIX AT THIRD

> **Gnawing through dried meat, you meet**
> **something poisonous.**
> **Small is distressed and confused.**
> **This is not a mistake.**

Biting through the obstacles between you and your Friend, you encounter something old and nasty. Take it on. Don't try to hide it. If you simply adapt, you will be ashamed and confused. Bring it out into the open. This is not a mistake. *Direction*: Clarify the situation. Be warm and insightful. Don't be afraid to act alone. You are connected to a creative force.

NINE AT FOURTH

> **Gnawing through parched meat with bones.**
> **You acquire a metal arrow.**
> **Divination: this drudgery is advantageous.**
> **The Way opens.**

Getting through this confrontation is a long, arduous task, but you will find something of great value. The drudgery will definitely be worth it in the end. This will open the Way for you, your Friend and the relationship. The effects will be lasting. *Direction*: Take things in. Be open and provide what is needed.

Six at Fifth

> **Gnawing through parched meat.**
> **Acquiring bronze and gold.**
> **Divination: adversity.**
> **This is not a mistake.**

Getting through this confrontation with your Friend is a long, arduous task. In the end you acquire something of very great value, wealth and the possibility to establish a line of descent. You are going to have to confront your own ghosts and shadows in the process. Have no fear, this is not a mistake. *Direction*: Disentangle yourself. Proceed step by step. Gather energy for a decisive new move.

Nine Above

> **Why are you locked in a wooden stock**
> **So your ears disappear?**
> **The Way closes.**

You keep trying to run everyone's life. This time you have seriously cut yourself off. You may have lost your relationship with your Friend. Why can't you hear this? You certainly won't accomplish anything this way! *Direction*: A fertilizing shock is coming. Re-imagine your situation. Gather energy for a decisive new move.

賈 ䷕ 22 Adorning PI

Beautify, embellish; display courage and beauty; elegance; make appearance reflect inner worth.

SETTING THE STAGE

You are not allowed to unite and climax without first considering your relationship. Thus there comes the time of Adorning. Accept this. Do not fear. Adorning means creating a face for things. Adorning begins without an expression.

OPENING THE FIELD

Adorn, PI: embellish, ornament, beautify; grace and elegance; inner worth that shines in appearance; energetic, brave, eager, passionate; display of courage. The ideogram links worth and beauty. It suggests a procession to bring home the bride, decked with flowers and festivity.

THE RESPONSE

Adorning will give you Success.
Small has an advantage in having a place to go.

Adorning describes your relationship, or your part in it, in terms of a display of courage and beauty. The way to deal with it is to beautify and embellish the way things are presented. You must attract each other and the world. Put on a brave and an elegant show. Let your appearance reflect your inner worth and the changes in your life. These are the festivities leading to a marriage. Be elegant. Be brilliant. Be brave. It will bring you success. If you can adapt to things and not impose your will, having a plan will help you.

SYMBOL, REFLECTION AND PRACTICE

Fire below Mountain. Adorning. An outer limit articulates inner brightness through display. This can release bound energy, freeing you from tension and compulsion.

Reflection: Value the chance for comfort and things of beauty. Turn your home or shared space into expressions of your inner worth and the way you value yourselves and each other. Allow yourself to shine in all that you do. Share your strength and elegance with others. Celebrate your union publicly. Beautify yourself to attract a partner, if you are seeking one. Show yourself as you are in all your fullness. Joyful union with your lovers or Friends is an outward demonstration of inner beauty. Delight in the being you are, as you delight in the being of your Friend. Other people in your life are important as well. Make sure that you maintain those connections. Add your Friend to your life and avoid replacing your life with your Friend.

Practice: Sit still regularly and concentrate on beautifying yourself within. Value what you notice, and notice all life and creativity in you. Repeat, "I am love; I am joy; I am beauty". Experience the infinite supply of these energies and share them with the world.

Transforming Lines

INITIAL NINE

Adorn your feet.
Put away your chariot and go on foot.

Adorn yourself with your courage and independence. Make your own Way now. Don't take the easy Way out. *Direction*: Stabilize your desires. Things are already changing.

SIX AT SECOND

Adorn your growing beard and hair.

Be brave and patient. It will take time, but a new connection to a really superior person is already there. If you adorn yourself with elegance and patience, it will lift you into a better relationship. *Direction*: Collect your forces. Prepare for an active time. If you let yourself be led, you can realize hidden potential. The situation is already changing.

NINE AT THIRD

> **Adorn yourself as if you are soaking in this.**
> **Divination: the Way is perpetually open.**

Let this relationship impregnate you. This is the one. Don't try to bring it to an end. This can open the Way for you and all your descendants. *Direction*: Take things in. Be open and provide what is needed.

SIX AT FOURTH

> **Adorn it as a Venerable Being,**
> **ride it like the soaring white horse.**
> **That is not at all an outlaw. Seek a marriage.**

Attribute great wisdom and worth to your relationship and your Friend. They can carry you like the sacred flying horse. Your Friend is not trying to steal anything from you. This is a time for a marriage, not distrust. *Direction*: Spread light, warmth and clarity. Don't be afraid to act alone. You are connected with a creative force.

SIX AT FIFTH

> **Adorn the hilltop garden.**
> **The roll of silk is little, very little.**
> **Distress and confusion,**
> **Bringing this to completion opens the Way.**

You are asked to become a formal member of your Friend's family circle. You must offer something at the family shrine, but you have very little to give. Go through with this, even though you are embarrassed, for it will open the Way. Soon you will have great cause to rejoice. *Direction:* Find supportive friends. Gather energy for a decisive new move.

Nine Above

White adorning.
This is not a mistake.

White is the color of what is plain, clear and pure. Don't hide things in this relationship. Bring out what is important. It is necessary to know the truth here, no matter what it costs. This is not a mistake. *Direction:* Accept the difficult task. It releases bound energy and delivers from sorrow. The situation is already changing.

剝 ☰ *23 Stripping* PO

Strip away old ideas, eliminate what is outmoded or worn out.

SETTING THE STAGE
Because this actually involved embellishing, success was used up. Thus there comes the time of Stripping. Accept this. Do not fear. Stripping means there is someone who strips things. Stripping means something is rotten.

OPENING THE FIELD
Strip, PO: flay, peel, skin, scrape away; remove, uncover, take off; reduce to essentials, diminish; prune trees, slaughter animals. The ideogram suggests taking decisive action to cut something away.

THE RESPONSE
Stripping, it is not advantageous to have a direction to go.

Stripping describes your relationship, or your part in it, in terms of outworn habits and ideas. The way to deal with it is to strip away what has become unusable and harmful. This brings renewal. Expression, feeling and rituals are worn out in your relationship. If you don't strip away the old and find the essentials underneath all may soon be over. This is the time to get rid of compulsive reactions, habits and ideas. Cut into the problem decisively. It won't do you any good to simply make plans. This is a time to work on yourselves. The old cycle is ending and a new one is being prepared. You can find a real creative balance with your Friend if you can get rid of all the old rationalizations.

This is a pivoting phase, where change can occur quickly and fundamentally. If you want to alter your relationship, apply yourself now.

SYMBOL, REFLECTION AND PRACTICE

Mountain resting on Earth. An old cycle is stripped away in the outer world, while inside the new is preparing. This reveals a whole new field of action.

Reflection: You have reached a time of change with each other. Do what is necessary to clear away what no longer works for you. Remove all but the essentials. A new era can dawn for you both, provided you do this. No blame is helpful here. Come to know what is important to you both. The core to core connection that you made with each other at the beginning is the root of your relationship. Time adds duties, habits and responsibilities in layers over this. Expose your core connection again by removing the layers, then your relationship can flourish. You don't need to know in advance where you will finish up. Involve your heart and keen perception in what you do. Be kind to each other. The rest will follow.

Practice: Sit and notice your breathing. Each time you breath in, incandescent, profoundly quiet and serenely sweet energy flows into you. At the end of your in-breath, hold very briefly to allow the energy to spread into every part of you. Then, as you breathe out, all that is inessential, unhelpful, limiting or contracting flows out too. Continue until only your essential beauty, strength and life remains.

Transforming Lines

INITIAL SIX

Strip the bed by using your stand.
Ignoring this divination closes the Way.
This is not an exorcism.

You have to confront the question of deeper intimacy in this relationship. It isn't working now. Take a stand. This is important. If you simply ignore the message, the Way will close. Don't turn your Friend into a ghost to be gotten rid of. *Direction*: Take things in. Be open and provide what is needed.

SIX AT SECOND
> **Strip the bed by marking things off.**
> **Ignoring this divination closes the Way.**
> **This is not an exorcism.**

You have to confront the question of deeper intimacy in this relationship. It isn't working now. Mark things off clearly. This is important. You may be associating with the wrong people. Don't turn your Friend into a ghost to be gotten rid of. If you simply ignore the message, the Way will close. *Direction*: Don't act out of ignorance. Wait and be sure. Something significant is returning. Be open and provide what is needed.

SIX AT THIRD
> **Strip it away!**
> **This is not a mistake.**

The time is now. Do it! By taking decisive action you can renew yourself and your relationship. This is not a mistake. Don't be sidetracked. *Direction*: Articulate the limits. Release bound energy. The situation is already changing.

SIX AT FOURTH
> **Stripping the bed, you slice close to the flesh.**
> **The Way closes.**

You are getting carried away with the renovation of your emotional life. You are about to do yourself and your Friend serious harm. This is not what the time is about. Pull back, let go for now, or you may see yourself all alone. *Direction*: You will emerge and be recognized. Re-imagine the situation. Gather energy for a decisive new move.

Six at Fifth

> **Thread the fish by the gills.**
> **You obtain the favor of the palace women.**
> **There is nothing for which this will not**
> **be advantageous.**

Pull things together in this relationship now. There is profit and fertility hidden in the stream of events. The palace women confer their grace and favor. Use your connections and trust your imagination. Anything is possible. There is nothing that will not benefit from the connection you are making now. *Direction*: Let things be seen. Strip away old ideas. Be open and provide what is needed.

Nine Above

> **A ripe fruit not eaten.**
> **The Relating Person acquires a cart.**
> **Small People can only strip their faces.**

You have stripped away the outmoded from this relationship and found the new. Now take in the fruits of your actions. Move on, carry it all away with you. Don't go back to your old way of relating. It would be like painting your house to avoid moving. *Direction*: Be open and provide what is needed.

復 ䷗ *24 Returning* FU

Love and spirit return after a difficult time; renewal, rebirth, re-establish the relationship; go back to the beginning; new hope.

SETTING THE STAGE
You can't completely use things up. When you exhaust stripping above, things will reverse below. Thus there comes the time of Returning. Accept this. Do not fear. Returning means reversing.

OPENING THE FIELD
Return, FU: go back, turn back, come back; return to the starting point; resurgence, renaissance, rebirth; renew, renovate, restore; again, anew; the beginning of a new time.

THE RESPONSE

Returning will give you Success.
Let things go out and come in without affliction.
Your Friend comes. This is not a mistake.
The Way reverses and returns to you.
Return comes on the seventh day.
It is advantageous to have a direction to go.

Returning describes your relationship, or your part in it, in terms of re-emergence and rebirth. The way to deal with it is to go back to meet the energy as it returns, to protect it and nourish it. Everything is new again. Go back to meet this new spring, back to your original feelings. Return to the source. Don't try to control things now. Let them come and go as they please. Your Friend will be there to meet you. This is a time when your life turns round and opens up. You are returning to yourselves and to each other. The old cycle of time is complete and the new time ready to come forth. It is a good idea to have a plan for your new relationship. Be open to new ideas. You must nurture the new energy. Stir things up. Let things emerge without forcing them. Returning to the Way is the root of all virtue, love and power. In the act of returning, you can see the heart of Heaven and Earth.

This is a pivoting phase, where change can occur quickly and fundamentally. If you want to alter your relationship, apply yourself now.

SYMBOL, REFLECTION AND PRACTICE

Thunder in Earth. Returning. Rousing new energy germinates and opens a new field of activity. You can give everything a new shape and form.

Reflection: A chance to begin again has arrived. Celebrate the opportunity together. Re-visit your origins with each other. Remember your reasons for coming together in the first place. By sharing your hopes and dreams, and showing how you now want to be together, much will change easily. Now is a time for ease, so take advantage of it. Begin again. Notice your expanded possibilities and enjoy the fun and life that you share as you do. Reshape your lives together with confidence. Your being together is reasserting its power. Friends do face tough times with each other. Having survived a difficult time, remember the joyful connections you first made. Be clear about what you now want with each other and what sort of partnership you want. Come together again and celebrate your joining.

Practice: Imagine that you are standing hand in hand with your Friend, facing the dawn. As the sun rises in front of you, both of you are flooded with the light and life of a new day. Absorb this fully, then, turning together, enter your new life.

Transforming Lines

INITIAL NINE
> **Don't keep returning at a distance.**
> **Don't just see the cause for sorrow.**
> **The Way to the Source is open.**

You have been keeping your Friend at a distance, probably because of the pain that has come between you. Now is the time to let it go. Don't just think about it. Go to him/her. The Way is fundamentally open to you both. *Direction*: Be open and provide what is needed.

SIX AT SECOND
> **Relinquishing and returning.**
> **The Way is open.**

Things in your relationship have been at fairly high tension. Each of you are claiming what your think are your rights. Let it go. Relax your grip. Let things rest. Be unselfish and benevolent. The Way will open to you. *Direction*: An important connection is approaching. Be open and provide what is needed.

SIX AT THIRD
> **Urgent return. Adversity.**
> **This is not a mistake.**

It is essential that you get back to your Friend. You will confront danger with its roots in the past. Difficult though this may be, it is not a mistake. *Direction*: Accept the difficult task. Release bound energy. The situation is already changing.

SIX AT FOURTH
> **The center is moving, return alone.**

The center of your life is shifting. You relationship may not survive. Move with this shift. It returns you to yourself. You won't be sorry. You are following the Way. *Direction*: An energizing shock is coming. Re-imagine the situation. Gather energy for a decisive new move.

SIX AT FIFTH
**Rich and generous return, without a
cause for sorrow.**

As you go to meet your Friend and the time renews itself, give with open arms. You will meet the same qualities in return. You will have no cause to regret what you do. *Direction*: Give everything a place to grow. Strip away old ideas. Be open and provide what is needed.

SIX ABOVE
**Delusion returns. There will be
calamities and errors.
If you try to move your legions,
it will end in great destruction.
The Way closes for the city and its leader.
This will end in ten years of uncontrolled
chastisement.**

This relationship is in a state of delusion. The two of you are blinded by self-deception and infatuation. If you go on in this way, your hard won growth will be destroyed. It will take at least ten years to deal with the repercussions of this catastrophe. The Way is closed. Think about where this desire comes from. Whatever you do, don't act it out. *Direction*: Take things in. Be open and provide what is needed.

无妄 ☴ *25 Disentangling*
WU WANG

**Disentangle yourself; spontaneous, unplanned;
free from confusion; clean, pure.**

SETTING THE STAGE
You actually return to yourself, so you can become disentangled.
Thus there comes the time of Disentangling. Accept this. Do not
fear. Disentangling means you will not attract disaster.

OPENING THE FIELD
Dis-/Without, WU: not having any, devoid of.
Tangle, WANG: embroiled, caught up in, entangled, trapped,
deeply involved; vain, rash, reckless, brutal behavior; lie,
deceive; idle, foolish, futile, without foundation; disordered,
insane.

THE RESPONSE
**Disentangling will give you Fundamental Success
and an Advantageous Divination.
Correct yourself now
or you will make mistakes through faulty perception.
Then it will not be advantageous to have a
direction to go.**

Disentangling describes your relationship, or your part in it, in
terms of acquiring the capacity to act spontaneously and confidently. The way to deal with it is to free yourselves from
disorder, compulsion and vanity. Don't get entangled. If this is a
brand new connection, stay clear for now. If it is an ongoing
relationship, you must free yourselves from your compulsions,

afflictive emotions and past pain, things that make you unable to perceive what is actually there. In doing so, you will acquire the ability to act and to love each other spontaneously and confidently. Work at it. It can change the time. It will bring you what you want. Without this self-correcting, you will only go on making the same old mistakes. Let yourself be inspired by the spirit of Heaven. Then proceed step by step and, in the end, success will be your fate. If you get entangled in your own emotional mess, how could you do anything right?

SYMBOL, REFLECTION AND PRACTICE

Thunder moves below Sky. Disentangling. Connect your inner growth to the principle of Heaven. You can gradually achieve your goal.

Reflection: Great creativity is available to you both, provided you stay clear with each other and those around you. Freedom comes from releasing yourself from limiting feelings and perceptions. Communicate directly with each other to do this. Approach this process innocently, as little children do. Act from loving, trusting hearts. Take one thing at a time. Seek out new people while staying aware of the love and joy in your primary connection. Your challenge is to center in innocence, while using worldly maturity to establish freedom. Deal with the pull of past and its limiting patterns without letting them determine your actions.

Practice: Imagine that you and your Friend are sitting together. You are constrained by cords, filaments and tentacles of light, sound and feeling. Imagine that you are both opening yourselves to your essential spirit. You share this opening. Light, quiet and serenity flood from within each of you, meet between you, intensify and instantly release the constraints. You are both free.

Transforming Lines

INITIAL NINE
Without embroiling. Go on, the Way is open.

You can do what you wish to do in this relationship, counting on the fact that you will not get tied up in negative emotions. The coast is clear. The Way is open. *Direction*: Communication may be blocked. Proceed step by step. Gather energy for a decisive new move.

SIX AT SECOND
"Don't till the crop, don't clear the land."
If you don't do these things,
It is advantageous to have a place to go.

This is not the time or place to work on your relationship. If you let things emerge spontaneously your plans will bring you success. Move on together. What you want is around the corner. *Direction*: Proceed step by step. Go your own way. Find supportive friends. Gather energy for a decisive new move.

SIX AT THIRD
Even in disentangling, there is a disaster.
Perhaps there are some tethered cattle.
If the moving people take them,
It is the capital people's disaster.

Even though you are quite without blame, you have lost something in your relationship that you care about. It feels like it was simply taken away. Understand that you can see your loss in two ways. If you identify with the capital people who stay in place, it is a disaster. If you identify with the moving people who are on their way to a new place, you actually acquire new strength.

Take your pick. *Direction*: Unite for a common goal. You are coupled with a creative force.

NINE AT FOURTH
An enabling Divination: this is not a mistake.

Whatever you are contemplating with your Friend, go through with your plan. This is an enabling divination. You are not making a mistake. *Direction*: Increase your efforts, pour in more energy. Strip away old ideas. Be open and provide what is needed.

NINE AT FIFTH
Even without embroiling, you are afflicted.
If you don't use medicine, you will soon rejoice.

You are suffering because of your Friend and your relationship. Though you may be in pain, don't treat this as a literal problem. See it imaginatively and spiritually and it will clear up. You will soon have cause to rejoice. *Direction*: Bite through the obstacles. Re-imagine the situation. Gather energy for a decisive new move.

NINE ABOVE
Even disentangled, it is an error to make a move.
No direction is advantageous.

Even though you are not caught up in negative emotions, there is nothing you can do for now. Leave your Friend alone. No plan you could make will help you. *Direction*: Follow the flow of events. Proceed step by step. Gather energy for a decisive new move.

大畜 ☰ 26 *Nurturing the Great* TA CH'U

Concentrate, focus on one idea; accumulate energy, support, nourish; bring everything together; great effort and great achievement.

SETTING THE STAGE
Becoming disentangled lets you nurture things. Thus there comes the time of Nurturing the Great. Accept this. Do not fear. Nurturing the Great means this is the right time to act.

OPENING THE FIELD
Nurture, CH'U: take care of, support, tolerate, encourage; help one another, overcome obstacles; tame, train; domesticate, raise, bring up; gather, collect, hoard, retain. The ideogram shows the fertile black soil of a river delta.
Great, TA: big, noble, important; focus on a goal, lead or guide your life; able to protect others; yang energy.

THE RESPONSE
**Great Nurturing will give you an
Advantageous Divination.
Don't eat in your dwelling or with your clan.
The Way is open.
It is advantageous to step into the Great River.**

Nurturing the Great describes your relationship, or your part in it, in terms of nurturing a central idea or purpose that defines what is valuable. The way to deal with it is to focus on a single idea that can concentrate your feelings and impose a direction on your lives. Center everything in your relationship around this goal or ideal. Gather together all your memories and experiences. This will bring both of you profit and insight. Don't stay in your immediate circle of friends or experiences. Reach out. This generates meaning and good fortune by releasing transformative energy. The doors are open to great things. Begin an enterprise or a project.

Symbol, Reflection and Practice

Sky in Mountain center. Nurturing the Great. The outer limit retains and nurtures Heaven's great force. Let yourself be led. You can realize your hidden potential.

Reflection: Dedicate time and attention to your Friend. Everything you do to build a future together will bring great rewards. Seek each other out away from family and friends. This is a time to collect yourselves and unify with each other, to develop and nurture inner strength and resources as a pair. You may be on the brink of a great new venture. Take the plunge with confidence. Pay primary attention to the way your deepest connection is prompting these opportunities. Regularly open your awareness to the deep importance of your Friend. Let this importance keep you focused when busy with your other activities.

Practice: Sit still and quiet for a few minutes. While you do, go inside as deeply as you can. Do this by traveling into your experiences of serenity, quietness, transparency and refined sweetness. Look at these experiences, listen to them, or feel them. You may increasingly dissolve, become silent, or go transparent. Allow this and commit yourself to oneness with the ultimate union from which everything flows.

Transforming Lines

Initial Nine

There is adversity.
It is advantageous to bring this to an end.

This relationship is heading into danger. It is haunted by old angry ghosts. The best thing to do is stop this now. In time you will understand what happened. *Direction*: Renovate a corrupt situation. If you let yourself be led, you can realize hidden potential. The situation is already changing.

NINE AT SECOND
The cart's axles are loosened.

You are quarreling with your Friend, so the cart can't go anywhere. The relationship has broken down. You need a show of beauty and bravery to release the bound energy. *Direction*: Beautify things and be brave. Release bound energy. The situation is already changing.

NINE AT THIRD
Pursuing a fine horse.
Divination: this drudgery is advantageous.
Say it this way: you are escorting an enclosed cart
and hidden cargo.
It is advantageous to have a direction to go.

You are pursuing your ideal of a relationship, but it is very difficult. Don't lose heart, the drudgery will bring you profit and insight in the end. Think of it this way: you are escorting a covered cart with your secret treasure inside. Having a plan will help you. *Direction*: Present hardship is future gain. Diminish passions and attachments. Something important returns. Be open and provide what is needed.

SIX AT FOURTH
A stable for young cattle.
The Way to the Source is open.

Your relationship is accumulating the force to carry heavy loads and confront difficult situations. This takes time. Don't give up now, the Way is fundamentally open. In the end you will have cause to rejoice. *Direction*: Abundance is coming. Be resolute. You are connected to a creative force.

SIX AT FIFTH

> **A gelded boar's tusks.**
> **The Way is open.**

Together, you have managed to confront and disable what could have been a powerful enemy. The obstacle is gone. The Way is open. This will bring rewards in the end. *Direction*: Accumulate Small to achieve the Great. Turn conflict into creative tension. The situation is already changing.

NINE ABOVE

> **Could this be Heaven's highway? Success.**

You two are on the right track. You are walking Heaven's highway. There is no doubt about your success. *Direction*: A flourishing and productive time is coming. If you let yourself be led, you can realize hidden potential. The situation is already changing.

頤 ䷚ 27 Jaws/ Nourishment YI

Nourishing and being nourished; take things in; the mouth, daily bread; speaking, words.

SETTING THE STAGE

Beings accumulate, then you must nourish them. Thus there comes the time of Jaws. Accept this. Do not fear. Jaws means nourishing. Jaws means correcting the source of nourishment.

OPENING THE FIELD

Jaws, YI: jaws, mouth; source of nourishment; take in, swallow, digest; eat; feed, sustain, nourish, support, bring up; what goes in and out of the mouth. The ideogram shows an open mouth.

THE RESPONSE

Jaws. Divination: the Way is open.
View the jaws. Seek the origin of what really fills
your mouth.

Jaws describes your relationship, or your part in it, in terms of nourishing and being nourished through both food and words. The way to deal with it is to become aware of where and how you are nourished and nourish others. This is the focus of your relationship, where the nourishment comes from and where it goes. Concern yourself with taking things in, metaphorically and literally. Help nourish each other's hopes and dreams. This generates meaning and good fortune by releasing transformative energy. Contemplate deeply what nourishes people and what you are nourishing. Think about what you give and what you ask for. Seek the source of what goes in and out of the mouth, for the answer to your question lies there.

Symbol, Reflection and Practice

Thunder in the Mountain. Jaws. Previous accomplishments nourish germinating new energy. You can give shape and sustenance to all things.

Reflection: Evaluate what you say and do with each other. Just as your Friend is a source of soul food for you, so you are for your Friend. Check that you are nourishing in what you share, that you offer tenderness, love and your primal reality. Allow yourself to experience the value in what you are sharing. When helpful, change how you are and what you do with each other. Find the source of true nourishment within and share this with each other. Nourish all of value around you, too. Take care with what you do, as what is given attention will flourish. Restraint in some areas may be needed, new approaches in others.

Practice: Sit still for a few minutes. Imagine that you and your Friend are embracing. As you do, imagine that your core to core connection intensifies. The unique balm that each of you is to the other spreads to fill you both. As your energies merge, you experience a wondrous expansion and fulfillment.

Transforming Lines

Initial Nine

> You simply put away your magic tortoise and say:
> "View my jaws hanging down". The Way closes.

When you confront the problems in this relationship, you simply give up and fall into self-pity. You put your soul and your imagination aside. So of course the Way closes. This sort of attitude has no value at all. *Direction*: Strip away your old ideas. Be open and provide what is needed.

SIX AT SECOND

Toppling the jaws.
Rejecting the canons and moving to the hilltop shrine.
Chastising the jaws closes the Way.

The source of nourishment in your relationship is disturbed. Don't follow all the rules. Move to the place where you feel secure. Even though this is a difficult time, don't try to punish people or put them in order. That would only close the Way. *Direction*: Diminish passions and involvement. Something important returns. Be open and provide what is needed.

SIX AT THIRD

Rejecting the jaws. Divination: the Way closes.
Like this you won't be able to act for ten years.
There is no advantageous direction.

You reject the hand that feeds you. The Way is definitely closed. If you go on like this, you will be paralyzed for ten years. There is nothing that you can do in this relationship. You idea goes against the Way. *Direction*: Beautify things. Release bound energy. Deliver yourself. The situation is already changing.

SIX AT FOURTH

Toppling jaws.
A tiger observes, glaring, glaring.
Pursuing, pursuing his passions.
This is not a mistake.

The source of nourishment in your relationship is disturbed. Search out the new with the ferocity and passion of a tiger. Be full of force and concentration. This extreme energy is not a mistake. It brings light and clarity to the situation. *Direction*: Bite through the obstacles. Re-imagine the situation. Gather energy for a decisive new move.

Six at Fifth

> **Rejecting the canons.**
> **Divination: staying where you are opens the Way.**
> **This does not let you step into the Great River.**

You are rejecting the rules most people live by in this relationship. The Way is open if you stay where you are and don't start any big projects for now. What you feel in doing this, however, is entirely correct. It will connect you with a higher ideal. *Direction*: A fertile new time is coming. Strip away old ideas. Be open and provide what is needed.

Nine Above

> **Nourished at the source. Adversity, the Way is open.**
> **It is advantageous to step into the Great River.**

You and your Friend are nourished by what came before you, an inheritance or legacy or perhaps simply your upbringing or your history. Now these things have come back to haunt you. Have no fear, the Way is open. The best way to deal with these doubts is launch into a brand new enterprise. Your relationship will be rewarded if you do. *Direction*: Something significant is returning. Be open and provide what is needed.

大過 ☰☰ *28 Great Traverses*
TA KUO

A crisis; gather all your strength; hold onto your ideals.

Setting the Stage
If your situation is not nourishing, you can't rouse things to action. Thus there comes the time of Great Exceeding. Accept this. Do not fear. Great Exceeding means toppling things over.

Opening the Field
Great, TA: big, noble, important; focus on a goal, lead or guide your life; able to protect others; yang energy.
Traverse, KUO: go across, surpass, overtake, overgo; get clear of, get over; cross the threshold, surmount difficulties; transgress the norms, outside the limits.

The Response
> **Great Traverses, the ridgepole is sagging.**
> **It is advantageous to have a direction to go.**
> **This will give you Success.**

Great Traverses describes your relationship, or your part in it, in terms of how to act in a crisis, a time of transition. The way to deal with it is to push what you truly believe beyond ordinary limits and accept the consequences. Have no fear. You and your Friend will have to stand together or you will fall apart. No half measures. The normal structure of things is sagging to the breaking point. Don't be afraid to act alone. Find your ideals and principles and don't compromise. Have a noble purpose and have a plan. There is a creative purpose in this breakdown. You will soon find it out. If your situation does not nourish new growth, then push it over and leave. This can be a very important time.

Symbol, Reflection and Practice

Mists submerge the Ground. Great Traverses. Inner penetration and outer stimulation create an intense concern with one great idea. You have access to great creative energy.

Reflection: Your relationship, or something important to you both is over strained. Inner strength cannot long be supported by what you currently have in place. A solution must be found. Partnerships are composed of two people, each with the responsibility and the strength to act. Shared responsibility comes from the separate willingness of each of you to commit to forthright action. You need to change what you do to use your shared power in your lives. Figure out what to do and follow through. Face the possibility that your new beginning could be either with or without each other. Go further than you normally would. This is a time for asserting your principles strongly. As you act, keep the welfare of everyone paramount. A complete restructuring of your lives may be required.

Practice: Sit still and stay quiet. Go inside, examine your strengths and how you have been using them. When you find power inside, go deeply into it and imagine that it flows from you into the world around you, finding the best path into the world. Allow yourself to ride the flow and observe the path it takes. Do something each day to change what you usually do.

Transforming Lines

Initial Six
Offer a sacrifice using a mat of white thatch-grass.
This is not a mistake.

Prepare your move very carefully. Think about your motives. Be clear and pure with your Friend. This is not a mistake. The beginning is humble, but the result will be great. *Direction*: Be resolute. You are connected to a creative force.

NINE AT SECOND
A withered willow gives birth to a shoot.
An older husband acquires a younger woman consort.
There is nothing for which this will not
be advantageous.

In the midst of the crisis, something happens to your relationship that gives it a whole new lease on life. This will benefit everything. *Direction*: This connects what belongs together. It couples you with a creative force.

NINE AT THIRD
The ridgepole buckles. The Way is closed.

The structure of your life together buckles and fails. There is nothing you can do to brace it up. The Way closes. *Direction*: Don't let yourself be isolated. Find supportive friends. Gather energy for a decisive new move.

NINE AT FOURTH
The ridgepole crowns the house. The Way is open.
If you try to add more, there will be distress
and confusion.

You have come through the crisis. The structure of your life together is strengthened and crowned with love and joy. The Way is open. You have all you need. If you try for more, you will only see distress and confusion and lose what you have. *Direction*: Understand your situation in terms of common needs and basic order. If you let yourself be led, you can realize hidden potential. The situation is already changing.

NINE AT FIFTH
> **A withered willow gives birth to flowers.**
> **An older wife acquires a young noble as husband.**
> **Without mistakes, without praise.**

As the crisis passes, something happens to your relationship that gives it a brief burst of beauty. There is neither blame nor praise involved. Enjoy it. It may soon be over. *Direction*: Continue on. Be resolute. You are connected to a creative force.

SIX ABOVE
> **If you exceed stepping into this water,**
> **You may submerge the top of your head.**
> **The Way closes.**
> **This is not a mistake.**

This relationship is in deep and troubled waters. You have to decide how much you want to get involved. If you do more than get your feet wet, chances are you'll be swept away. This is not a matter of fault. Something significant is involved. Be clear and choose. You have to decide. *Direction*: Be resolute. You are connected to a creative force.

坎 ☵ 29 Repeating the Gorge HSI K'AN

Collect your forces, confront your fears, take the plunge; practice, repeat, rehearse; rise to the challenge.

SETTING THE STAGE

You are not allowed to bring exceeding to completion. Thus there comes the time of Gorge and danger. Accept this. Do not fear. Gorge means falling and taking the risk. Gorge means what is below.

OPENING THE FIELD

Repeat, HSI: practice, rehearse, train; again and again; skilled; repeat a lesson; drive, impulse. The ideogram shows thought carried forward by repeated movements.

Gorge, K'AN: dangerous place; hole, pit, cavity; steep precipice; snare, trap, grave; rushing water; critical time, test, key point; take the risk without reserve.

Gorge is one of the Eight Helping Spirits. He is the moistening one. He rewards those suffering in the pit. As a spirit guide Gorge leads through danger. He dances with ghosts, risks all and always comes through. He exults in work, he dissolves all things. He is a black pig, hidden riches.

THE RESPONSE

> Repeating the Gorge. Danger.
> There is a connection to the spirits.
> Hold your heart fast. This will bring you Success.
> Making a move brings you honor.

Repeating the Gorge describes your relationship, or your part in it, in terms of confronting danger and difficulty. The way to deal with it is to take the risk without holding back. You cannot avoid this, alone or together. Face your fears and take the risk, like water that falls into a pit, fills it and flows on. Practice, train, get ready. This is a critical point that could trap you both, so give it everything you have. You are connected to the spirits and they will help you. Hold your heart fast. Choose the time and make the move.

This is a pivoting phase, where change can occur quickly and fundamentally. If you want to alter your relationship, apply yourself now.

SYMBOL, REFLECTION AND PRACTICE

Repeating Gorge. The stream flows on, toiling and taking risks, dissolving the differences in its path. You can nourish yourself and the ones you care for.

Reflection: You or what you share is in danger. Facing it is best, as it will keep returning until you take care of it. Risk is high. You have things to say and do with each other. Find your courage by acting while feeling frightened. Find what you need to do inside your heart, as you open your awareness to what you face. Stay true to your heart and keep expressing it with everything that arises. Persist. Your persistence will shift the dangerous momentum in the end. Act internally, too. Directly face the inner reality of what seems to threaten you. Give priority to finding ways of dealing with this on the inside. Your inner solutions can show you the way to proceed externally.

Practice: Each day, sit still and quiet for a few minutes. Imagine that you are filled with love by encouraging it to flow from your heart into the rest of your body. Bring what you most fear with your Friend into your awareness. Think about what you are most reluctant to face. Submerge yourself in the feelings, thoughts, perceptions, impulses and desires that arise as you do. Experience them fully. Then, using all your senses, concentrate on the physical world underneath and around you. Keep doing this until you return to equilibrium. When you finish, do something, even if small, to deal with what you are facing.

Transforming Lines

INITIAL SIX

Repeating Gorge.
Entering the pit in the Gorge.
The Way is closed.

By responding in the same way again and again, you and your Friend get caught in a dead end. This is the pit of depression and melancholy. Don't get caught here. It closes the Way. *Direction*: Set limits. Find your voice. Take things in. Be open and provide what is needed.

NINE AT SECOND

Venture into the Gorge.
Seek and acquire through the Small.

Venture into danger. You will get what you need in this relationship by being flexible and adaptable. Have modest goals, don't impose your will and you will succeed. *Direction*: Change who you associate with. Strip away old ideas. Be open and provide what is needed.

SIX AT THIRD

Gorge after Gorge is coming at you.
Soften your desire to venture into danger.
Don't get trapped in the pit in the Gorge.

Relax and pull back. What is coming is more than you can handle right now. If you push on, you will get trapped in the pit, a fatal diversion. Are you sure you know what you want in this relationship? Think about your values. *Direction*: If you let yourself be led, you can realize hidden potential. The situation is already changing.

SIX AT FOURTH

> **A cup, liquor, add a platter and use a jar as a drum.**
> **Let in the bonds that come from the window.**
> **Complete this! This is not a mistake.**

If you are trapped or cut off from your Friend, don't fight it. Lay out an offering, give of yourself. Open the window and let the spirit in. You are right on the border, the place where events emerge. Go through with your plans. This is not a mistake. *Direction*: Move out of isolation. Find a supportive group. Gather energy for a decisive new move.

NINE AT FIFTH

> **The Earth Spirit is appeased.**
> **This is not a mistake.**

There has been enough danger. The spirits are appeased. Go on with your relationship. Don't do too much. Don't fill it to overflowing. Don't make a grand effort. Be content with what is there. *Direction*: Organize your forces. Something important is returning. Be open and provide what is needed.

SIX ABOVE

> **Tied with stranded ropes.**
> **Sent away to the Jujube Grove for judgement.**
> **For three years you will get nothing.**
> **The Way closes.**

You have committed a serious transgression against your Friend. You are bound and judged. There is no way out of this very unpleasant situation. You will simply have to serve your time. *Direction*: Dispel illusions! Take things in. Be open and provide what is needed.

離 ䷝ *30 Radiance* LI

**Light, warmth, awareness; join with, adhere to; articulate
and spread the light, see clearly.**

SETTING THE STAGE

Falling will have a place to come together again. Thus there must
come the time of Radiance. Accept this. Do not fear. Radiance
means coming together. Radiance means what is above.

OPENING THE FIELD

Radiance, LI: light, illuminate, discriminate; put things in order;
consciousness, awareness; brightness, fire, warmth; leave, step
outside the norms, separate yourself; two together, encounter
someone; belong to, adhere to, depend on. The ideogram shows
a magical bird with brilliant plumage.

Radiance is one of the Eight Helping Spirits. She is the shining
one. She connects things. She reveals herself in the omens. As a
spirit guide Radiance is the bright presence of things. She leads
through her warm clear light, through beauty and elegance, the
radiance of living beings holding together. She is the bird dancer
with brilliant plumes and brings strange encounters and lucky
meetings. She is nets and soft things with shells. She is a bright
pheasant, bird of omen.

THE RESPONSE

**Radiance will give you Success and an
Advantageous Divination.
Accumulate female cattle. The Way is open.**

Radiance describes your relationship, or your part in it, in terms
of light and warmth, awareness and coherence. The way to deal
with it is to articulate and spread the light, awareness and

connection. You and your Friend need to experience the warmth, light and awareness that come from depending on each other. In this way you can accumulate the receptive strength that can carry burdens. This will bring you success and a deep connection. This connects things. It will bring together what belongs together. Be gentle and clear in spirit. Spread your warmth and awareness. Connect and illuminate things.

This is a pivoting phase, where change can occur quickly and fundamentally. If you want to alter your relationship, apply yourself now.

SYMBOL, REFLECTION AND PRACTICE

Light, warmth and awareness spread, bringing together those who belong together. Radiance. You can build up great inner power.

Reflection: Plan time together. When together, celebrate your rightness with each other. Talk about your feelings, share what you value about each other. Put this into words and deeds. Do at least three things a day that directly express and celebrate your shared sense of light, harmony and joy. Spend time alone centering and exploring the source of your personal radiance. Encourage it to fill you physically, emotionally and cognitively. Your spiritual being is showing. Express it by making yourselves available to each other and sharing the great beauty that lies within each of you. Anything you share intensifies. In the midst of the atmosphere you create, take advantage of the abundant radiance to adjust things that need changing. Melt them in the warmth of what you share, instead of trying to engineer them into a different form.

Practice: Imagine sitting on the Earth in vast indigo blue space. The sun is on your right and the moon on your left. Imagine the two coming together so they encompass you. Experience the beauty of this radiant blending. Follow the prompts it gives you in what you do.

Transforming Lines

INITIAL NINE

Treading, then polishing.
Respect it! This is not a mistake.

You are just beginning a relationship. Be very careful with the first steps. Polish and clarify your motives and feelings. Treat this beginning and your Friend with real respect. You won't be making a mistake. *Direction*: A transition. Be Small and careful. Search outside the norms. Don't be afraid to act alone. This connects you with a creative force.

SIX AT SECOND

Yellow radiance.
The Way to the Source is open.

You have found the connection. Light and power from the Earth's center radiates through you and your relationship. The Way is fundamentally open. *Direction*: A creative, blossoming time is approaching. Be resolute. You are connected with a creative force.

NINE AT THIRD

The setting sun's radiance.
If you don't beat on a jar, drum and sing,
You will lament like a very old person.
The Way closes.

Instead of spreading light and warmth in your relationship, you see everything in the light of the setting sun. You don't beat your drum and your sing your songs. Instead, you lament all the terrible things that have happened in your life together. Why go on like this? Get a grip on yourself. *Direction*: Bite through the obstacles! Proceed step by step. Gather your energy for a decisive new move.

NINE AT FOURTH

It assails you when it comes.
It burns up. It dies away.
Throw it out.

This relationship is a flash in the pan. It comes on strong, burns out and dies. Throw it away. It has no place in your life. *Direction*: Put on a happy face. Re-imagine the situation. Gather energy for a decisive new move.

SIX AT FIFTH

Tears gush forth in streams.
Sadness breaks out in lamentation.
The Way is open.

It feels as if you have lost a connection with someone important to you. Cry and mourn. Let your sadness be seen. This will open the Way again and bring your Friend to their senses. *Direction*: Find supportive friends. You are coupled with a creative force.

NINE ABOVE

The King sets out on an expedition.
There will be an excellent result.
Sever the head, leave the demons absolutely alone.
This is not a mistake.

This is a time to take aggressive measures. Something has been harming your relationship and now you must deal with it. Be determined and aggressive. You will have excellent results. However, take what is important and let the rest go. This is not a mistake. Opposition will fall apart. *Direction*: A time of abundance is coming. Don't be afraid to act alone. You are coupled with a creative force.

Part II: Relations

Part II of *Symbols of Love* is the Book of Relations. It begins with attraction and marriage (Symbols 31 and 32). It moves through several pivotal phrases: the circulation of energy (Symbols 41 and 42); action and stillness (Symbols 51 and 52); penetration and expansion (Symbols 57 and 58); and the continual renewal of the Way (Symbols 63 and 64).

Each of these Symbols represents a place where things can change quickly and fundamentally. These are the times to apply yourself if you want to alter your relationship, for better or for worse. In the text, the Symbols are indicated by a box:

> This is a pivoting phase, where change can occur quickly and fundamentally. If you want to alter your relationship, apply yourself now.

咸 ䷞ *31 Conjoining* HSIEN

Excite, stimulate, influence; strong attraction; bring together what belongs together.

SETTING THE STAGE
From the relations of Sky and Earth come the myriad beings. From the relations of the myriad beings come woman and man, wife and husband, child and parent, server and leader, above and below. Accept this. Do not fear. This is a new beginning. Conjoining means urging things on.

OPENING THE FIELD
Conjoin, HSIEN: Excite, stimulate, influence, mobilize; strong attraction, connection; bring together what belongs together; make contact; move, trigger; all, totally, universal; unite, conjunction (as planets); literally: a broken piece of pottery, the two halves of which are used to identify partners.

THE RESPONSE
> **Conjoining will give you Success**
> **and an Advantageous Divination.**
> **Embracing the woman opens the Way.**

Conjoining describes your relationship, or your part in it, in terms of a strong attraction, a real influence that triggers you into action. The way to deal with it is to find the best means to bring what is separated back together. This is the energy that brings things together, a sudden attraction, a surge of energy that can create deep connections and lasting relationships. Be open to it and further it. Reach out. Let yourself be moved. Don't be afraid to open up and let the feelings take hold. Embrace the power of the woman and the yin. This generates meaning and good fortune by releasing transformative energy. This attraction can give you a way to order your heart and everything you are doing.

> This is a pivoting phase, where change can occur quickly and fundamentally. If you want to alter your relationship, apply yourself now.

SYMBOL, REFLECTION AND PRACTICE

Mists above Mountain. Conjoining. Inner stillness supports stimulation and joy. If you let yourself be led, you can realize hidden potential.

Reflection: The full benefit of men and women together in all combinations is available now. Enjoy as you share. This time is about receptivity to each other, gentle, joyous strength. Look to the woman in your relationship and in yourself for guidance on what is important and how to act. If you seek a relation, take the feminine way. Rather than 'going on the hunt', stop and make yourself available to what is coming. Strong forces are moving to bring people together. Act in this way and the shape of things in your life will change.

Practice: To help you see what to do, regularly imagine that you and your partner are both women, whether or not you are physically. In this imagined relationship, observe the way both of you live your lives with each other. Ask what advice these two have for you and open yourself completely to their answers.

Transforming Lines

INITIAL SIX

It conjoins your big toe.

You feel the first stirrings of creative desire. The influence is just beginning. There is no telling what will happen. This impulse

could change the way you see your relationship. *Direction*:
Revolution and renewal. You are coupled with a creative force.
Use it well.

SIX AT SECOND

<blockquote>

It conjoins your calves.
The Way closes.
Stay where you are and the Way will open.

</blockquote>

Don't get swept off your feet. A hasty move will lead to nothing
but trouble. Stay right where you are and you'll soon have what
you want. *Direction*: Don't be afraid to act alone. You are connected to a creative force. Use it well.

NINE AT THIRD

<blockquote>

It conjoins your thighs.
Hold onto your following!
Going on brings distress and confusion.

</blockquote>

You are in danger of becoming obsessive. This will do you no
good. Hold onto yourself and what supports you. If you go on
running after this connection, you will simply be covered in distress. *Direction*: Gather resources for a great new project. Proceed
step by step. Gather energy for a decisive new move.

NINE AT FOURTH

<blockquote>

Divination: the Way is open.
The cause of sorrow disappears.
You waver back and forth, things come and go.
Your partners will simply follow your thoughts.

</blockquote>

Express your affection. This is a very favorable influence. Your
sorrow over the past will simply disappear. The Way is open.
You go back and forth in your thoughts, trying to understand this
new feeling. Have no fears. Your Friend will be there for you.

Direction: Re-imagine the situation. Gather energy for a decisive new move.

Nine at Fifth

> **It conjoins your neck.**
> **No cause for sorrow.**

This is a very deep affection that will endure over time. You are feeling the beginnings. This will wipe away past sorrows. *Direction*: A transition. Be very Small. Don't be afraid to act alone. You are connected to a creative force. Use it well.

Six Above

> **It conjoins your jaws, cheeks and tongue.**

This influence inspires you to talk to your friend. You burst forth in passionate speech. It may not last long, so be ready to retreat when words run out. *Direction*: Pull back. It will connect you with a creative force. Use it well.

恆 ䷟ *32 Persevering* HENG

**Continue, endure; constant, consistent, durable;
self-renewing; a stable married couple.**

SETTING THE STAGE
The Way of husband and wife is not allowed not to last. Thus
there comes the time of Persevering. Accept this. Do not fear.
Persevering means lasting.

OPENING THE FIELD
Persevere, HENG: continue on, endure and renew the Way; constant, consistent, continue in what is right; continue in the same
spirit; stable, regular, enduring, perpetual, self-renewing; ordinary, habitual; extend everywhere, universal; the moon that is
almost full. The ideogram shows enduring on the voyage of life.

THE RESPONSE

Persevering will give you Success.
This is not a mistake.
This is an Advantageous Divination.
It is advantageous to have a direction to go.

Persevering describes your relationship in terms of what contin-
ues and endures. The way to deal with it is to seek and work at an
enduring union. Renew your decision and your commitment
each day. Endure in your connection and your passion. This is
not a mistake. This will bring success, profit and insight to your
relationship. It will bring you to maturity. Make a plan together
and follow it. Put your ideas to the trial. This is the Way of husband and wife, a Way that must endure over time. Cling to your
principles. Let the end of each day be the start of a new one.

This is a pivoting phase, where change can occur quickly and fundamentally. If you want to alter your relationship, apply yourself now.

Symbol, Reflection and Practice

Thunder and Wind. Persevering. Inner penetration and outer arousal continually renew each other. You can act clearly and decisively.

Reflection: You are getting it right. To maximize this, each of you needs to ensure that you are making the contribution that is unique to you. This produces the right balance. Regularly take time to imagine yourself with your Friend. Then imagine the two of you blending into one person, producing a person who is a fusion of you both. Notice what this person does and the way it is done. It is deep decisions that bring people together, not just the external factors that might seem compelling. Realize the power of this deep level with each other. Whether you are with a Friend or want one, live by your principles, continually testing them by exposing them to introspection. Follow through with each other. Accept that change and building something desirable takes time. Persist for years, one step at a time, if this is what is necessary.

Practice: Deliberately and consciously renew your decision to be with your partner each day. Do it repeatedly throughout the day. Decide, "I am here; I am continuing".

Transforming Lines

Initial Six

Deepening and persevering.
Divination: the Way closes.
There is no advantageous direction.

You are going into this relationship too deeply, too soon. This is the wrong way to go about it. The Way is closed. Nothing you come up with can help you. *Direction:* The strength is there. Let the situation mature. Be resolute. Together you are connected to a creative force. Use it well.

NINE AT SECOND
The cause of sorrow disappears.

If you persevere in what you have established, your cares and sorrows will disappear. Commit yourself to your Friend. The power and the ability are there. *Direction:* Be very Small at the beginning. Don't be afraid to act alone. You are connected to a creative force. Use it well.

NINE AT THIRD
Not persevering in your power and virtue.
Perhaps you receive a gift,
even then you are embarrassed.
Divination: distress and confusion.

You are betraying your own promise. Everything will lead to your embarrassment, because you cannot keep your heart sincere. Come now. Surely you can do better than this. *Direction:* Release bound energy. The situation is already changing.

NINE AT FOURTH
The fields without game.

There is simply nothing in sight, no possibility of a real relationship. The best thing to do is to leave quietly. Then you may find what you need. *Direction:* Make the effort. If you let yourself be led, you can realize hidden potential. The situation is already changing.

SIX AT FIFTH
>   Divination: Persevere in your power and virtue.
>   The Way opens for the wife and her people.
>   The Way closes for the husband and son.

Persevere in your own virtue. This is a time to make a choice
about your relationship. If you can act as a wife, things will open
up in this situation. If you choose the husband's way, you will cut
things off. Be supportive and receptive. *Direction:* A transition.
Don't be afraid to act alone. You are connected to a creative
force. Use it well.

SIX ABOVE
>   **Rousing persevering, the Way closes.**

You won't make anything happen like this. Too much excitement and agitation, trying to drum up support from your Friend
that is not there. Why not quieten things down and try to find
an image of what has you so upset? *Direction:* Find a vessel, an
image of transformation, and use it. Be resolute about this. It will
connect you with a creative force. Use it well.

迸 ☰☷ *33 Retiring* TUN

Withdraw, conceal yourself, pull back; retreat in order to advance later.

SETTING THE STAGE
You are not allowed to last and stay in your place. Thus there must come the time of Retiring. Accept this. Do not fear. Retiring means withdrawing.

OPENING THE FIELD
Retire, TUN: withdraw, conceal yourself, retreat; pull back in order to advance later; run away, flee, escape, hide; disappear, withdraw into obscurity; secluded, anti-social; fool or trick someone. The ideogram shows luck and wealth through withdrawing.

THE RESPONSE
Retiring will give you Success.
This is an Advantageous Divination if you can be Small.

Retiring describes your relationship, or your part in it, in terms of conflict and withdrawal. The way to deal with it is to pull back and seclude yourself in order to prepare for a better time. The present situation is doing you no good, so withdraw and stay concealed for now. Don't seek to impose your ideas or desires. If you can adapt to what is going on, while at the same time detaching yourself from events and strong emotions, you will have success, profit and insight. Disentangle yourself. You need time alone, time to think and ground yourself. Once you get free of the current confusions and illusions, you will be able to think things through and prepare for a better time. Decline involvement, refuse invitations, keep things at a distance. Use integrity, avoid using resentment and hatred. Immerse yourself in your own work. You will know when the time changes. In the long run this can completely change your relationship, for the better.

SYMBOL, REFLECTION AND PRACTICE

Sky below the Mountain. Retiring. An inner limit draws creative energy into retirement. A passionate connection. This will bring you together.

Reflection: It is time to stay still, to make yourself quiet, to reflect, to pull back and to reduce the contact you have with each other. This is not a time for sorting things out. The things that you might want to change are too powerful to deal with in their present form. It is a time to regroup internally. However, active presence is required, not passivity. You withdraw, but stay connected. Take time to build your inner strength while waiting for the right moment to act overtly again. Regularly sink into the center of your being. Notice your breathing and sink further in with each outward breath. Keep going until you rest on the solid foundation of your core and in the clear light of understanding. Build what you need from there. Your withdrawal may prompt who need to act, to do so.

Practice: Each day imagine a perfect resolution. Include in your fantasy a re-balancing of strength and the development of openness between everyone. Imagine all involved act with mutual respect, cooperation and love.

Transforming Lines

INITIAL SIX

Retiring at the tail, adversity.
Do not act, but have a direction to go.

You and your Friend get caught in old plans and old promises. You can't cut through this yet. Be ready. Have a plan to use when you get a chance. *Direction*: Find supportive friends. You are coupled with a creative force. Use it well.

Six at Second

Held by a yellow cow's skin.
Absolutely nothing can succeed in loosening this.

You are caught. You won't shake these things loose. Face it. They belong with you. You are going to have to work with these plans and your Friend. *Direction:* You are coupled with a creative force. Use it well.

Nine at Third

Tied retiring. Affliction and adversity.
Accumulate servants and concubines to open the Way.

You and your Friend are entangled in a web of difficulties, duties and connections, you can't get out of this alone. Let others help you as servants (who carry out orders) and concubines (who create a pleasant mood). Then you can begin to put it all at a distance. *Direction:* Proceed step by step. Gather energy for a decisive new move.

Nine at Fourth

Love through retiring.
The Relating Person opens the Way.
Small People are obstructed.

Love comes through retiring. Think about what you care for. It will open the Way. Keep greedy people at a distance now. *Direction*: Proceed step by step. Gather energy for a decisive new move.

Nine at Fifth

Excellence through retiring.
Divination: the Way is open.

Excellence comes through retiring. It will open the Way for loving connection and give you a lot to do. Have no regrets. The Way is open. *Direction*: Search on your own. Don't be afraid to stand alone. You are coupled to a creative force. Use it well.

NINE ABOVE
> **Wealth and fertility come through retiring.**
> **There is nothing that is not advantageous.**

By retiring, you bring wealth and fertility to everything around you. You are doing exactly what is needed for the relationship and will be very successful at it. *Direction*: This is a significant influence. It will couple you with a creative force. Use it well.

大壯 ☰☰ *34 Invigorating the Great* TA CHUANG

Great invigoration, a great idea; focus, drive, advance; injury, wound, harm.

SETTING THE STAGE

You are not allowed to completely retire. Thus there comes the time of Invigorating what is Great. Accept this. Do not fear. To Invigorate the Great, you must first still yourself.

OPENING THE FIELD

Great, TA: big, noble, important; orient your will towards a self-imposed goal; ability to lead your life; yang energy.

Invigorate, CHUANG: inspire, animate, strengthen; strong, robust, vigorous, mature; damage, wound, unrestrained strength. The ideogram shows a strong, stout man.

THE RESPONSE

Invigorating the Great gives you an Advantageous Divination.

Invigorating the Great describes your relationship, or your part in it, in terms of strength, drive and invigorating power. The way to deal with it is to focus this strength through a great idea held in common. You have great strength and the ability to make things grow. If you keep on, your relationship can flourish. But you must focus this strength through a central idea that benefits both of you. Engage yourself passionately. Use the great powers you have. However, be careful! Your strength and drive have the capacity to harm people too.

SYMBOL, REFLECTION AND PRACTICE

Thunder above Sky. Invigorating the Great. Inner force is directly expressed in action. Be careful. You can act clearly and decisively.

Reflection: Many aspects are important in relationships. All need to be taken into account. Forthright action has its place, as long as timing and sensitivity to the needs and vulnerabilities of others are properly considered. So in this time of great strength, remember to consider the likely reactions others will have to you. Each day, discuss with each other what you will do on your joint projects. Emphasize the skills and creativity that you can each contribute and how to remain alert to the sensitivities of everyone else involved. Keep the balance as your strength mounts. Channeling your strength and energy into defined goals will help you to ground yourselves.

Practice: Regularly imagine that every cell in your body is filled with radiant light, great strength and beautiful harmony. Every thought, feeling and action is imbued and aligned with these properties. See this energy spreading to others in exactly the ways required for all to benefit. Act accordingly.

Transforming Lines

INITIAL NINE

**Invigorating the feet.
Chastising closes the Way.
There is a connection to the spirits.**

You are out to conquer the world. Hold back just a moment. Don't try to tell your Friend what to do and don't set out on any adventurous expeditions. The spirits are with you, but start slowly. *Direction*: Continue on. Be resolute. You are connected to a creative force. Use it well.

NINE AT SECOND
>Divination: the Way is open.

Whatever you want to do will be successful. This begins a flourishing time in the relationship. *Direction:* A time of abundance. Don't be afraid to act alone. You are coupled to a creative force. Use it well.

NINE AT THIRD
>Small People invigorate things now.
>The Relating Person uses the empty spaces of a net.
>Divination: adversity.
>The he-goat butts a hedge and entangles his horns.

You are trying to catch something. Don't force it. Use strategy and an open heart rather than aggression with your Friend. You are confronting some troublesome past experiences. If you use force, like the stubborn goat, you will only get yourself entangled. *Direction:* If you let yourself be led, you can realize hidden potential. The situation is already changing.

NINE AT FOURTH
>Divination: the Way is open.
>The cause for sorrow disappears.
>The hedge is broken through,
>And there is no more entanglement.
>Invigorate the axles of your great cart.

The obstacle vanishes and together you can do what you want. The past simply disappears. There is nothing holding the two of you back. Put your shoulders to the wheel and do the great things that are in you to do. *Direction:* A great and flourishing time approaches. If you let yourself be led, you can realize hidden potential. The situation is already changing.

SIX AT FIFTH

> **Loses the goat and changes.**
> **Without a cause for sorrow.**

Let go of forward drive. Change your considerable strength into imagination. Don't always charge into obstacles. There are more interesting ways to deal with your relationship now. If you realize this, your sorrows will simply disappear. *Direction:* Be resolute. You are connected to a creative force. Use it well.

SIX ABOVE

> **The he-goat butts a hedge.**
> **He can't pull back and he can't push through.**
> **There is no advantageous direction.**
> **Accept the drudgery, and thus the Way will open.**

The relationship is stuck and you are in for a bit of hard work. You can't force your way out of this one. Just sit there and go through the painful analysis of your mistakes. As you do this, the Way will open of itself. *Direction:* Your hard work begins a better time. Be resolute. You are connected to a creative force. Use it well.

晋 ䷢ *35 Prospering* CHIN

Emerge into the light; advance, be noticed; give and receive gifts; dawn of a new day.

SETTING THE STAGE

You are not allowed to simply bring invigorating to completion. Thus comes the time of Prospering. Accept this. Do not fear. Prospering means advancing. Prospering means emerging into the daylight.

OPENING THE FIELD

Prosper, CHIN: Emerge into the light; advance and be recognized; receive gifts; spread prosperity, the dawn of a new day; increase, progress; grow and flourish, as young plants in the sun; rise, be promoted; permeate, impregnate. The ideogram shows birds taking flight at dawn.

THE RESPONSE

> **Prospering like calm and stately Prince Kang,**
> **You acquire and bestow gifts of horses and benefits**
> **in multitudes.**
> **In one day you are received three times.**

Prospering describes your relationship, or your part in it, in terms of emerging into the light. The way to deal with it is to give your affection freely in order to let all things flourish. Delight in things. Your relationship has been hidden in the shadows. No longer. Now it is recognized and honored. You emerge together into the full light of day. There is no doubt about your advance. Be calm in the strength of your affection. Help others. Re-imagine the entire situation. You have the power now to bestow strength and spirit. Use what is given to help your Friend and your relationship. Let your care extend to everyone in need.

Symbol, Reflection and Practice
Brightness comes from Earth. Prospering. Light emerges from darkness, spreading prosperity to all. You can re-imagine a difficult situation.

Reflection: The tide has turned for you with your Friend. Move forward with it. You can do this with confidence, because the flow of the Way is reasserting itself in you both. What you have built already is strong. Honor this and keep developing it. At the same time, think creatively about new directions and styles. Regularly sit and imagine that your relationship was a chrysalis in a cocoon that is now emerging as a butterfly. It is coming into the light. Contemplate the beauty of its new form and do what is necessary to promote its full birth. Notice the transforming beauty in yourself and your Friend.

Practice: Each day, take time to consider your spiritual priorities. Encourage any action you take afterwards to arise naturally from your quiet time. Do nothing, rather than trying to impose your will or continuing to act from habit. Specifically commit to do to at least one thing a day that expresses these priorities.

Transforming Lines

Initial Six
You prosper and are held back.
Divination: the Way is open.
There is a net of relationships that connects
you to the spirits.
You will be enriched. This is not a mistake.

At the beginning of your emergence you are held back. Don't worry. You are connected to a net of spiritual connections. This situation will ultimately enrich your relationships. It is definitely not a mistake. *Direction:* Bite through the obstacles. Re-imagine the situation. Gather energy for a decisive new move.

SIX AT SECOND

You prosper yet are apprehensive.
Divination: the Way is open.
Accept this close-woven chain mail
And the blessing of the Royal Mother.

You set out in this relationship, but then feel anxious and sorrowful. Don't worry. The Way is open. Take on this difficult task and receive the Royal Mother's blessing. *Direction:* Gather energy for a decisive new move.

SIX AT THIRD

The crowds are sincere.
The cause for sorrow disappears.

Your Friend has confidence in you. Don't hold back. Give of yourself unstintingly. Your sorrows will vanish. *Direction:* Begin your travels. Don't be afraid to act alone.

NINE AT FOURTH

You prosper like a bushy-tailed rodent.
Divination: adversity.

As you and your Friend prosper together, you are set upon by greedy people and bad memories. Don't act like a timid little mouse. Throw these old ideas away. Don't give up what you know is right. *Direction:* Strip away old ideas. Be open and provide what is needed.

SIX AT FIFTH

> The cause for sorrow disappears.
> Letting go or acquiring, have no cares.
> Go on, the Way is open,
> There is nothing that is not advantageous.

All your sorrows will vanish. Don't worry about anything, simply give yourself to your relationship and the work it involves. The Way is open and the time is right. Everything will benefit from this endeavor. *Direction*: Change who you associate with. Proceed step by step. Gather energy for a decisive new move.

NINE ABOVE

> Prospering with your horns.
> Hold fast and subjugate the capital. Adversity.
> The Way is open. This is not a mistake.
> Divination: distress and confusion.

You are trying to control the relationship by force. Deal with your own troubles first. You have to confront the negative images you have of things, which are based on past experience. This is difficult, but it opens the Way. If you don't try, you will find yourself covered in confusion. *Direction*: Gather energy in order to respond when the call comes. Re-imagine the situation. Gather energy for a decisive new move.

明夷 ☷☲ *36 Hiding Brightness* MING YI

Hide your light; protect yourself; accept and begin a difficult task; hidden influences.

SETTING THE STAGE

When you advance you will inevitably come to a place where you are injured. Thus there comes the time of Hiding Brightness. Accept this. Do not fear. Hiding means injury. Hiding Brightness means being an outcast.

OPENING THE FIELD

Hiding Brightness, MING YI: Hide your light, protect yourself; begin a difficult task; marginalized, outcast; also, a bird of omen, announcing danger or misfortune.

Hide, YI: keep out of sight; distant, remote; raze, lower, level; ordinary, plain; cut, wound, destroy, exterminate; barbarians, vulgar uncultured people. The ideogram shows a man armed with a bow.

Brightness, MING: light from fire, sun, moon and stars; awareness, intelligence, consciousness; understand, illuminate, distinguish clearly; lucid, clear, evident; symbolized by the bright bird, a golden pheasant. The ideogram shows sun and moon.

THE RESPONSE

Hiding Brightness. Divination: drudgery is advantageous.

Hiding Brightness describes your relationship, or your part in it, in terms of the need to protect yourself and accept a difficult task. The way to deal with it is to dim or conceal your aware-ness and intelligence by voluntarily entering what is beneath you, like the sun as it sets in the evening. Make no mistake, you are definitely in danger. Dim your light and pretend to be ordinary. You can avoid injury and find a release from this situation. Accept drudgery. Hide yourself in the work at hand. This is a time to begin something new if you can accept the work and loneliness involved in being out there all by yourself. Your deliverance is already being prepared. It can begin a new time.

SYMBOL, REFLECTION AND PRACTICE
Brightness enters the Earth center. Hiding Brightness. Hide your inner brightness by joining the common Earth. You can be deliv-ered from danger and tension.

Reflection: Concentrate on external, day-to-day activities. These will keep you well grounded in the world as you deal with whatever is threatening you. Stay internally centered in your light and creativity, and keep them to yourself. Make yourself one with what you need to protect yourself from, by imagining that you have become it. This will activate the equivalent danger in you that you are now projecting outside. By digesting the danger you find within, you will release your-self from any apparent danger on the outside. Then you will be more able to deal with the situational danger safely and clearly.

Practice: Sit still regularly and go into the core of your experience. Go to that part of you that observes everything, the "I" inside you. When centered in this "I", cultivate the awareness that the people and situations surrounding you don't determine who you are and what you do. You are free to decide. Meditate on an ideal outcome that opens the Way for all.

Transforming Lines

INITIAL NINE

> Hiding your Brightness through flight,
> Dipping your wings in the waters.
> The Relating Person must go three days
> without eating.
> Have a direction to go.
> Master your words to influence others.

You must escape together from an impossible situation. Have courage and stamina. Figure out a plan. You can convince people of anything if you master your words. *Direction*: Stay humble and connected to the facts. Trust hidden processes. Release bound energy. The situation is already changing.

SIX AT SECOND

> Hiding your Brightness. Hidden, hurt in the left thigh.
> Use a horse to rescue this,
> invigorating strength will open the Way.

This is a serious but not deadly wound to the relationship. You can deal with it. Mobilize your spirit. Come to your Friend's rescue. If you can invigorate your imaginative power the Way will open and you will free yourself and your relationship. *Direction*: A flourishing time is coming. If you let yourself be led, you can realize hidden potential. The situation is already changing.

NINE AT THIRD

> Hiding Brightness in the Southern Hunt with dogs.
> You acquire their Great Head.
> Divination: you will not be afflicted.

In the midst of very considerable difficulties, you find the central illusion that is causing this chaos. This will release your relationship from the pain and sadness that afflicts the two of you. It lets you open your heart once more. *Direction*: Something important returns. Be open and provide what is needed.

SIX AT FOURTH

> **Enter the left belly.**
> **Catch the heart of the hidden brightness.**
> **Issue forth from their gate and chambers.**

Get out of this terrible place. Take aggressive action. Go right to the heart of it and reclaim your lost intelligence. Leave this relationship and don't come back. *Direction*: This begins a time of abundance. Don't be afraid to act alone. You are connected with a creative force. Use it well.

SIX AT FIFTH

> **Prince Chi hides his brightness.**
> **Advantageous Divination.**

The two of you must pretend to be a part of this situation. Don't lose your integrity. You will survive. This will bring you profit and insight in the end. Be clear about what is really happening. *Direction*: The situation is already changing.

NINE ABOVE

> **Not brightening but darkening.**
> **First he mounted to Heaven,**
> **Then he fell to the Earth.**

Finally the darkening ends and you are free. This whole situation has hurt your relationship. Can you understand why? Would you act like this yourself? It is time for a bit of self-examination. *Direction*: Renovate a corrupt situation. The situation is already changing.

37 *Dwelling People*
CHIA JEN

Hold together, family, clan, intimate group; support, nourish, stay in your group; people who live and work together.

SETTING THE STAGE
When you are injured in the outside world, you inevitably turn back to your dwelling. Thus there comes the time of Dwelling People. Accept this. Do not fear. Dwelling People means being on the inside.

OPENING THE FIELD
Dwelling People, CHIA JEN: A group of people living and working together; hold together, intimate; nourish, support; family, clan. **Dwell**, CHIA: home, household, family, relations, clan; a business, a school of thought; master a skill; have something in common. The ideogram shows the most valued domestic animals, the pig and the dog.
People, JEN: an individual person; all human beings, humanity. The ideogram shows people kneeling in submission or prayer.

THE RESPONSE
Dwelling People. Divination: the woman is advantageous.

Dwelling People describes your relationship, or your part in it, in terms of the support provided when you live and work with others. The way to deal with it is to care for those sharing your dwelling place and your activities. Think of yourself as part of a family with ties of feeling and a sense of shared responsibility.

Take care of the dwelling and what is within. Nourish the shared feelings and the sense of a bond that supports you. Act through the feminine and the yielding power of the yin, rather than through masculinity and the aggressive yang. Nourish and care for things. Spread warmth and light. Stay inside the net of feelings. Be receptive to and protective of your Friend. Be clear about your positions and worth in this relationship. This can set your world right.

SYMBOL, REFLECTION AND PRACTICE

Wind originates from Fire and issues forth. Dwelling People. Inner warmth and clarity penetrate the world, bringing people together. You can collect energy for an important new move.

Reflection: The center of the family is the husband and wife. When they function well, the family does too. Put your energy into making sure that each of you is getting and doing what is needed. Draw from this strong base and provide your strength to them. Meditate on the woman as the holy ground on which the family stands and in which its members grow. Without this ground, the family cannot exist. Meditate on the man as a holy, tender gardener, who, adoring the ground for its richness, nourishes it further and tends all that grows in it. Make dedicated time available for each other. Arrange regular family meetings where everyone attends. Eat together at least once a day, if at all possible. Make these things amongst your highest priorities.

Practice: Regularly contemplate nature for inspiration on how to live with your family. Watch birds and animals tend their young and spend time with each other. Notice the balance of this, how sometimes family needs take precedence and at other times the couple's do. Observe the natural order of things and consider how to apply it to your own life.

Transforming Lines

INITIAL NINE
Through enclosing there is a dwelling.
The cause for sorrow disappears.

Stay inside your group of acquaintances with your Friend. Don't take chances now. Your sorrows will disappear. You are not ready to act yet. *Direction*: Proceed step by step. Gather energy for a decisive new move.

SIX AT SECOND
Release what you have to give without
a plan or direction.
Locate yourself in the center and feed your people.
Divination: the Way is open.

You and your Friend are the center of this group. Give open-handedly. Don't impose yourself on anyone. Help and nourish the others in your group. This will open the Way for all of you. *Direction*: Accumulate Small to achieve the great. Turn conflict into creative tension. The situation is already changing.

NINE AT THIRD
Dwelling people, scolding, scolding.
Free yourselves from the causes of sorrow and adversity.
The Way opens.
Wife and son, giggling, giggling.
Going on like this brings distress and confusion.

Make sure your house is in order and that you and your friend know your places and roles. Don't just let things slide by. The confrontation isn't easy, but facing old habits will open the Way. This calls for honest repentance of past mistakes. If you simply let things go, everything will be confused. Take charge! Articulate relations clearly. *Direction*: Increase your efforts. Pour in more. A fertile time is coming. Strip away old ideas. Be open and provide what is needed.

SIX AT FOURTH

An affluent dwelling.
The Way of the Great is open.

Goodness, riches and happiness will flow in this dwelling. The Way is open. Make this abundance serve a real purpose. There is the challenge of your relationship. *Direction*: Bring people together. Take action. You are coupled to a creative force. Use it well.

NINE AT FIFTH

The King approaches the Ancestral Temple
to receive blessings for all.
Care for all the beings opens the Way.

You can create a world around you like a temple or a house of the spirit. Act from your heart. Try to help others. Your care for your Friend and the ones you love will open the Way. *Direction*: Adorn the house with beauty. Release bound energy. The situation is already changing.

NINE ABOVE

You have a connection to the spirits that
impresses others.
Bringing this to completion opens the Way.

Whatever you want to do together is possible. You have the spirit and the intelligence to carry all before you. Act on your desires. Do what you need to do. The Way is open. *Direction*: The situation is already changing.

膵 ䷥ *38 Diverging/ Outcast* K'UEI

Opposition, discord, conflicting purposes; outside the norm, strange meetings, the ghost world; change conflict to creative tension through awareness.

SETTING THE STAGE

When the Way of Dwelling is exhausted, you inevitably turn away. Thus there comes the time of Diverging. Accept this. Do not fear. Diverging means turning away.

OPENING THE FIELD

Diverge, K'UEI: opposition, discord; change conflict into outcast, outside the norm; wilderness, the spiritual world; creative tension; separate, oppose, move in opposite directions; distant, remote from each other; animosity, anger; astronomical opposition, 180° apart yet connected by a common axis.

THE RESPONSE

Diverging, the Small's affairs open the Way.

Diverging describes your relationship, or your part in it, in terms of opposition, conflict and alienation. The way to deal with it is to change this conflict into a creative tension through a shift in your awareness. You and your Friend seem to be moving in different directions. The relationship is tied up by conflict and discord. The way to deal with this situation is to adapt to each thing that happens and not try to impose your will. This generates meaning and good fortune by releasing transformative energy. You will be able to see things clearly and turn your differences into creative tension. You have to be able to both join things and to separate them. Diverging implies turning away from the ordinary and encountering what is outside your normal range of experience. Think about things from a new perspective. If you understand both what links people and what separates them, you can connect your situation with something great.

SYMBOL, REFLECTION AND PRACTICE
Fire rises, Mists descend. Diverging. Inner stimulation and outer radiance can be held in creative tension. The solution to the problem is already on its way.

Reflection: The tendency for differences to push or pull people apart is expressing itself here. The creative challenge for you is to accept this current reality and find ways of connecting the apparent opposites. Each of you has something to contribute. The important questions are: what is it? and how will you do it? To discover your answers, practice holding both sides of every issue or situation in your awareness at the same time. Hold your hands with your palms facing up, imagining, as you do, that each one holds one side of the situation you are considering. Allow them to settle there and to interact freely. Notice how this brings apparent opposites together, often in a new form. Act from the fusion of the two parts, rather than from their separation.

Practice: Spend time regularly contemplating carefully the situation you face. In particular, identify any shared patterns, any similarities, ways of joining, any harmony or common ground, between the apparent opposites. Each day, do something in the situation that affirms and promotes unity while recognizing difference.

Transforming Lines

INITIAL NINE
**The cause for sorrow disappears.
If you lose your horse, do not pursue it.**

It will return to its origin in your heart.
If you see hateful people, make no mistakes.

Don't try to prove your point. Don't worry over what seems gone. Let it all go. Harmony, strength and love will return by themselves. The pain and sorrow you feel will vanish. It is vital that you don't let your own or your Friend's negativity poison your mind. Keep your thoughts warm and clear and you will make no mistakes. *Direction*: Gather energy for a decisive new move.

NINE AT SECOND

You meet your lord in a narrow street.
This is not a mistake.

In an unexpected way, in an unexpected place, you meet a Friend who conquers your heart and makes everything clear. Don't be afraid. This is not a mistake. *Direction*: Bite through the obstacles! Gather energy for a decisive new move.

SIX AT THIRD

You see your cart pulled back
and your cattle hobbled.
Your people are struck down and their noses cut off.
What you initiate will not be completed.

This could be a serious setback, the end of your relationship. You have tried to force your way through and have met unexpectedly strong opposition. Nothing you start will come to fruition now. *Direction*: Clarify and brighten your central idea. Be resolute. You are connected to a creative force. Use it well.

NINE AT FOURTH

Diverging and alone.
You meet a fundamentally powerful man.
Mingling together connects you to the spirits.

Alone and feeling isolated by your own thoughts, you encounter something or someone inspiring. Don't be afraid. Joining with this force will put you in touch with the spirits. What you have in your heart for your relationship will come to pass. *Direction*: Diminish passion and past involvement. This is the return of something significant. Be open and provide what is needed.

SIX AT FIFTH

The cause for sorrow disappears.
Your ancestors eat the meats of sacrifice.
How could going on like this be a mistake?

Your relationship is blessed by your ancestors. They bite their way through this ordinary life to find you and confer their blessings. Your sorrows will soon vanish. There is no way in which this relationship can be a mistake. *Direction*: Proceed step by step. Find supportive friends. Gather energy for a decisive new move.

NINE ABOVE

Diverging and alone.
You see pigs covered with muck,
A chariot carrying dead souls.
First you stretch the bow, then you loosen the bow.
Those you are confronting are definitely not
outlaws, seek a marriage.
Going on you will meet the rain and thus the
Way will open.

Alone and isolated, you see your Friend as a dirty pig or a carload of ghosts. At first you are hostile, but then you relax. Where does this hostility come from? Your Friend is not trying to hurt you. Reach out and seek an alliance. As you begin, the falling rain will wash the past away and the Way will open. *Direction*: If your let yourself be led, you can realize hidden potential. The situation is already changing.

襲 ☷☶ 39 *Difficulties/ Limping* CHIEN

Obstacles, afflictions, feeling hampered; overcome difficulties by re-imagining the situation.

SETTING THE STAGE

Turning away inevitably involves hardship. Thus there comes the time of Difficulties. Accept this. Do not fear. Difficulties mean hardship.

OPENING THE FIELD

Difficulty, CHIEN: Obstacles, afflictions, blocks; to feel hampered; overcome difficulties by re-imagining the situation; limp, lame; weak, crooked, unfortunate. The ideogram shows cold feet and suggests a wrong attitude.

THE RESPONSE

> **Difficulties. The southwest is advantageous.**
> **The northeast is not advantageous.**
> **It is advantageous to see the Great Person.**
> **Divination: the Way is open.**

Difficulties describes your relationship, or your part in it, in terms of obstacles and feelings of affliction. The way to deal with it is to see through the difficulties and gather energy for a decisive new move. You are encountering what feels like an endless set of obstacles. Nothing is going right. You don't really have the strength to confront all this. Well, don't. Stop trying to be a hero. Retreat, pull back, open yourself to other people. Don't go on struggling alone. Talk to someone who can help you reflect on this situation. This generates meaning and good fortune by releasing transformative energy. It is how you are thinking about things that makes it all so hard. There is danger all around you. If you can see it and stop pushing on, you will understand what is happening. Correct the way you use power and change what you depend on. Re-imagine this situation. Then you will link your relationship with something great.

SYMBOL, REFLECTION AND PRACTICE

Gorge above Mountain. Difficulties. An inner limit blocks outer venture, giving rise to reflection and change. You can gather the energy to ford the stream of events.

Reflection: To deal with your difficulties, think about how you would like things to be. Affirm what you want within yourself and share this with your Friend. Everything you share is intensified and thus more likely to influence your lives. Seeking help from each other, or from others, is likely to help. Be prepared to contemplate your situation for some time. Then you will be able to act from a well established inner momentum that will take you in the direction in which you need to move.

Practice: Every day, sit for a few minutes and affirm "I am a perfect outcome". As you do, do your best to feel a certainty that your affirmation is true. Remain open to and ask for help from all available powers. Accept whatever you experience. Go about the business of your day, open to an emerging understanding of what is required.

Transforming Lines

INITIAL SIX

Difficulties going, praise is coming.

You are cut off from your Friend and feel frustrated. Resist the temptation to push your way through. If you wait and open

yourself to new thoughts, all these frustrations will disappear.
You will be praised for doing this. *Direction*: The situation is
already changing.

SIX AT SECOND
The King's servant, difficulties, difficulties.
Your own person is definitely not the cause.

You are pushing on through a sea of troubles in this relationship,
and you don't really know why everything is so complicated. Be
calm in your heart. The difficulties you are facing are not your
fault. You are truly called on to confront them. *Direction*:
Connect with common needs and strengths. Turn conflict into
creative tension. The situation is already changing.

NINE AT THIRD
Difficulties going, the reversal is coming.

Don't keep chasing what you want. Don't force the issue with
your Friend. If you just wait calmly, the whole situation will
reverse itself. Then you will truly have cause to rejoice. *Direction*:
Change who you associate with. Strip away your old ideas. Be
open and provide what is needed.

SIX AT FOURTH
Difficulties going, an alliance is coming.

You feel lonely and think your Friend is against you. But you are
beating your head against a brick wall. Relax. Your Friend is
looking for you right now and knows how valuable you are.
Direction: Open yourself to this influence. It couples you with a
creative force. Use it well.

NINE AT FIFTH
In Great difficulties, partners come.

In the middle of the greatest difficulties, when you are about to give up, a Friend arrives to help you. What you are doing is very important. Don't give up now. *Direction:* Stay humble and connected to the facts. Release bound energy. Dissolve obstacles to understanding. The situation is already changing.

SIX ABOVE
> **Difficulties going, ripeness is coming.**
> **The Way opens.**
> **It is advantageous to see the Great Person.**

If you try to impose your will in this relationship, your Friend will most certainly be unhappy. Let go and the solution will drop into your hand like a ripe plum. The relationship is full of promise, if you can only see it. Talk to someone who can help you reflect on what is going on. *Direction:* Proceed step by step. Gather energy for a decisive new move.

解 ☵☳ 40 *Loosening* HSIEH

**Solve problems, untie knots, release blocked energy;
liberation, freed from suffering.**

SETTING THE STAGE

You are not allowed to be completely exhausted by hardships.
Thus there comes the time of Loosening. Accept this. Do not
fear. Loosening means relaxing your grip.

OPENING THE FIELD

Loosen, HSIEH: Solve problems, untie knots, release blocked
energy; liberation, deliverance, free from suffering and constraint, dispel sorrow, solve problems, eliminate bad effects,
release blocked energy; divide, detach, untie, scatter, dissolve,
dispel; liberate, set free; analyze, explain, understand. The
ideogram shows a horn instrument used to untie knots.

THE RESPONSE

Loosening.
The southwest is advantageous.
If you have no further place to go, the return is coming.
The Way opens.
If you have a direction to go, begin at daybreak.
The Way opens.

Loosening describes your relationship, or your part in it, in terms
of deliverance, a release from tension and suffering. The way to
deal with it is to untie the tangles, sorrows and problems that are
binding you. Try to understand your motivations and the emotions that have produced this state of tension. Release the
blocked energy. Forget about the past. Untie the knots in your
soul and open yourself to new energy and passion. Don't hold

back. Celebrate the simple act of being alive. If you have nothing to do, wait for the return of the spirit. If you have things to do, start at first light and do them quickly. This generates meaning and good fortune by releasing transformative energy. This is a great and arousing time. Enjoy it together.

Symbol, Reflection and Practice

Thunder and Rain arousing. Loosening. Your inner world dissolves and releases rousing new energy. The action you desire is already underway.

Reflection: You can do a lot internally now. Make the most of the opportunity to guide your actions from inside. Meditate regularly that the light of Heaven is radiating from you and enlivening all within and around you. Do this with your Friend as often as possible. Imagine that your Way is now clear. If you are still struggling in your daily life, let go. Relax. Finish any unfinished business. Let go of any grudges. Prepare for a new era. You are connecting Heaven and Earth and the streams from both are mingling within you. Everything you touch will benefit.

Practice: Imagine daily that light and transparency, quietness and harmony, joy and sweetness have replaced all entanglements and cloudiness, noise and disharmony, unhappiness and bitterness. Specifically include your Friend and all others involved in your fantasy. Watch for change.

Transforming Lines

Initial Nine
This is not a mistake.

Act on your plans. Be vigorous. You are in exactly the right position with your Friend. This is not a mistake. *Direction:* Let yourself be led. You can realize hidden potential. The situation is already changing.

NINE AT SECOND

> **You catch three foxes in the fields**
> **And acquire a yellow arrow.**
> **Divination: the Way is open.**

Vigorously pursue your objectives. There are forces that seem to be threatening the relationship, but you catch them in the act and acquire their power. You have the ability to realize your desires. The Way is open. *Direction*: Gather energy in order to respond when the call comes. Re-imagine the situation. Gather energy for a decisive new move.

SIX AT THIRD

> **Bearing a burden yet riding in a carriage.**
> **This will attract outlaws in the end.**
> **Divination: distress and confusion.**

You are acting above or beneath yourself and either way it invites disaster for the relationship. Who you are trying to impress? Is it really worth it? If you go on like this, you will be covered in shame. *Direction*: Endure in what is right. Be resolute. You are connected to a creative force. Use it well.

NINE AT FOURTH

> **Loosen your thumbs.**
> **Partners will come in the end.**
> **Splitting apart brings a connection to the spirits.**

Leave your current relationship. It is doing you no good. A new Friend will come after a time of loneliness. The act of splitting away from what you now think is necessary will draw the spirits to you. Have no doubt about it. Act now. *Direction*: Organize your forces. Something significant is returning. Be open and provide what is needed.

Six at Fifth

> If a Relating Person is held fast,
> There will be loosening.
> The Way opens.
> There is a connection to the spirits.

If you are truly committed to your relationship, you will be freed from the constriction you feel in your present life and united with your Friend. Hold fast to what you believe. It opens the Way and connects you to the spirits. *Direction*: Look within to find the way out. Find supportive friends. Gather energy for a decisive new move.

Six Above

> The prince shoots a hawk on a high rampart above him.
> He catches it.
> There is nothing that is not advantageous.

You capture the force opposing your plans and desires for this relationship. Don't worry. Be brave. Attack now and you will most certainly win. This will begin a new cycle of time. Everything will benefit. *Direction*: Gather energy for a decisive new move.

損 ☴ *41 Diminishing* SUN

Decrease, sacrifice, loss; concentrate, diminish your involvement, decrease your desire; aim at a higher goal.

SETTING THE STAGE

Relaxing must necessarily let things go. Thus there comes the time of Diminishing. Accept this. Do not fear. Diminishing and Augmenting are the beginning of increase and decrease.

OPENING THE FIELD

Diminish, SUN: lessen, take away, make smaller, weaken, damage; lose, spoil, hurt, blame; offer in sacrifice, give up, give away, concentrate, aim at a higher goal. The ideogram suggests making an offering to the spirits.

THE RESPONSE

Diminishing will give you connection to the spirits.
The Way to the Source is open.
This is not a mistake.
This is an Enabling Divination.
It is advantageous to have a direction to go.
You ask how you can make use of this?
Two platters allow you to make the presentation.

Diminishing describes your relationship, or your part in it, in terms of the need for sacrifice and concentration. The way to deal with it is to decrease passionate involvement and free your-self from emotional entanglement. Let your fixed ideas go, mute your passions, restrain your desire, curb your anger. Diminish your personal connection. This makes energy available for new development. It will connect you with a spiritual dimension that you haven't yet been aware of. The Way to the source is open. Think about what you are doing why you are doing it. Then you can come up with a plan and follow it. Offer sacrifice to the spirit by using two platters. This means that you should decrease yang or aggressive energy and increase yin or receptive energy. This is an enabling or empowering divination. It is the beginning of a new increase to come. It generates meaning and good fortune by releasing transformative energy. It can repair your connection to each other. Diminish what is below and augment what is above. This will connect you to the time and the spirit.

> This is a pivoting phase, where change can occur quickly and fundamentally. If you want to alter your relationship, apply yourself now.

SYMBOL, REFLECTION AND PRACTICE

Mists below Mountain. Diminishing. An outer limit restricts involvement, stimulating inner development. You can return to the source of your love.

Reflection: You and your Friend need to shift gears. Your energies have been focused in the emotional stream and you need to re-center in the spiritual. Avoid repressing your feelings and passions in this process. Their energy is a powerful aid to lifting and expanding the level of your attention. To do this, stop briefly at regular times during the day. Concentrate on the point between your eyebrows. Internally look at, listen to, feel, or talk to yourself about the point. Touch it externally, if it helps you to focus. This point is a doorway from the world to spirit. Concentrating on it will help you to refine and transform all your energies. Open your inner eyes to everything, listen to it all, feel whatever is there. Notice what evolves. In this way, you can easily get another view, theme or feel for what is now needed.

Practice: Sit quietly and notice the point between your eyebrows. Pay close attention to it with all your inner senses.

Imagine that a small replica of you is sitting in there. Stay aware generally of your situation as you do. From time to time, pay attention to the Earth underneath you. Imagine yourself conducting highly refined spiritual energy through your body into the rest of your life and into the Earth beneath you.

Transforming Lines

INITIAL NINE
> Bring this affair to an end and go swiftly.
> This is not a mistake. Discuss diminishing it.

This involvement is a mistake. Leave now, quickly. Talk about how you can get out of the way. Don't let it diminish your resolve. *Direction*: There are hidden forces at work. This is the return of something significant. Be open and provide what is needed.

NINE AT SECOND
> Advantageous Divination.
> Chastising closes the Way.
> This diminishes nothing, it augments it.

This is a very advantageous relationship. Everyone will benefit. But it won't help if you try to discipline your Friend and set things in order. That will close the Way. This connection won't diminish things, it will augment them. *Direction*: Take things in and nourish them. Be open and provide what is needed.

SIX AT THIRD
> When there are three people moving,
> they will be diminished by one.
> When one person is moving, she will acquire a Friend.

If you are involved in a triangle, it will soon become a couple. If you are alone, you will soon have a Friend. *Direction*: A time for a great endeavor. Let yourself be led. You can realize hidden potential. The situation is already changing.

SIX AT FOURTH
Diminish your affliction.
Commission someone to carry the message swiftly.
There will be rejoicing.
This is not a mistake.

This relationship is seriously harming you. Diminish your involvement. Send someone quickly to give the message. Then you will have cause to rejoice. Have no doubts, this is not a mistake. *Direction*: Turn conflict into creative tension. The situation is already changing.

SIX AT FIFTH
Perhaps ten pairs of tortoise divinations
augment you.
Nothing can control or contradict you!
The Way to the Source is open.

What a fortunate answer! The Way is fundamentally open. Nothing can get in the way of your plans and your desires. The two of you will be showered with blessings. Enjoy it! *Direction*: Bring your inner and outer lives together. Take things in. Be open and provide what is needed.

NINE ABOVE
This diminishes nothing, it augments it.
This is not a mistake. Divination: the Way is open.
It is advantageous to have a direction to go.
You acquire servants, not a dwelling.

Your relationship will not be diminished but augmented. It will bring good things for both of you. The feelings you have now are not a mistake. They actually open the Way. Draw up a plan. Be sure of yourself. You will get considerable help, but this will not be a sedentary affair. *Direction*: An important connection approaches. Something significant returns. Be open and provide what is needed.

益 ䷩ *42 Augmenting* YI

**Increase, expand, develop, pour in more;
fertile and expansive.**

SETTING THE STAGE
Diminishing without end must augment things. Thus there
comes the time of Augmenting. Accept this. Do not fear.
Diminishing and Augmenting are the beginning of increase and
decrease.

OPENING THE FIELD
Augment, YI: increase, advance, expand, add to; benefit,
strengthen, support; pour in more, overflowing, superabundant;
restorative, fertile; useful, profitable, advantageous. The
ideogram shows a horn of plenty.

THE RESPONSE
> **Augmenting. It is advantageous to have a
> direction to go.
> It is advantageous to step into the Great River.**

Augmenting describes your relationship, or your part in it, in
terms of increase, advance and development. The way to deal
with it is to increase your passionate involvement and pour in
more energy. Give freely and openly, without reserve. Make a
plan together and follow it. Everything will benefit from your
passionate commitment. This is a very good time to start a
new project together. Through your work on your connection,
you have triggered a flourishing new time. Be like the rising
sun. Throw your old ideas away. Move with the flourishing
time.

This is a pivoting phase, where change can occur quickly and fundamentally. If you want to alter your relationship, apply yourself now.

SYMBOL, REFLECTION AND PRACTICE

Wind and Thunder. Augmenting. Rousing energy bursts from within to permeate the world. You can strip away your old ideas.

Reflection: Now you can reap the rewards of your previous restraints. Act purposefully to express what is important to the two of you. Set the time aside, both for planning your projects and for discussing what is necessary to complete them. Act confidently, passionately and vigorously with each other, always remembering to stay sensitive to your impact on others. Spend time singly or together imagining the full success of your endeavors and desires. What you share you intensify, so share with your Friend as often as you can to energize what you want.

Practice: On a daily basis, cultivate your awareness of the abundance of Heavenly energy and how available it is now. Actively seek and create ways of expressing this directly with others. Do something specific to express this at least three times a day.

Transforming Lines

INITIAL NINE

It is advantageous to arouse and activate the Great.
The Way to the Source is open. This is not a mistake.

Your relationship needs a purpose, a great idea around which you can organize yourselves and your passion. The Way is fundamentally open. It is the right time to act. Go forward. This is definitely not a mistake. *Direction*: Let everything come into view. Strip away old ideas. Be open and provide what is needed.

SIX AT SECOND
> **Perhaps ten pairs of tortoise divinations augment you.**
> **Nothing can control or contradict you!**
> **Divination: the Way is perpetually open.**
> **The King makes presentations to the Supreme Power.**
> **The Way is open.**

What a fortunate answer! Anything you and your Friend wish to do will prosper. The Way is open to your ideas, not just now, but in the future. Enjoy it! But remember the spirit in your happiness. Then the Way will truly be open. *Direction*: Bring your inner and outer lives into accord. Take things in. Be open and provide what is needed.

SIX AT THIRD
> **Augmenting affairs when the Way is closed.**
> **This is not a mistake.**
> **There is a connection to the spirits**
> **and the center is moving.**
> **Inform the prince. Use the scepter to speak.**

What seems like an unfortunate happening in your relationship will turn out to your mutual benefit. Act on your ideas. This is not a mistake. Tell your Friend what is happening. Insist on your right to speak. You are connected to the spirits and they will carry you through. *Direction*: Find supportive friends. Gather energy for a decisive new move.

SIX AT FOURTH
> **The center is moving.**
> **Inform the prince and adhere to him.**
> **It is advantageous to act. Depend on shifting the city.**

The center of your life is shifting. Stay loyal to your Friend. Act on your ideas. Depend on the fact that everything is changing.

Direction: Stay out of quarrels and wrangles. Proceed step by step. Gather energy for a decisive new move.

Nine at Fifth
> **You have a connection to the spirits and**
> **a benevolent heart.**
> **Don't question it, the Way to the Source is open.**
> **Say it like this: "A connection to the spirits and a**
> **benevolent heart are my power and virtue."**

Act through your virtue and kindness. You have a kind, generous heart and a noble spirit. Don't question this. Use it. The Way is fundamentally open. Your kindness and compassion are the way to create this relationship. *Direction*: Take things in. Be open and provide what is needed.

Nine Above
> **This absolutely does not augment you.**
> **Perhaps your Friend will smite you.**
> **You establish your heart without persevering.**
> **The Way closes.**

You are being fickle, wayward, perhaps deceitful toward your Friend and towards yourself. Nothing good can come of this. Don't play with people. The Way will close and you will be left open to danger. *Direction*: Articulate the limits. Strip away old ideas. Be open and provide what is needed.

夌 ☰ 43 Deciding/Parting
KUAI

Resolution, act clearly, make a decision and announce it; breakthrough; part from the past, separate; clean it out and bring it to light.

SETTING THE STAGE

Augmenting without end must break through. Thus there comes the time of Deciding and Parting. Accept this. Do not fear. Deciding means breaking through. The strong breaks through the supple.

OPENING THE FIELD

Decide, KUAI: choose; resolute, decisive, act clearly; breakthrough, critical moment; prompt, certain, clear; clean out a wound, bring something to light; separate, divide, cut off, divide in two; parting of two rivers, parting of the ways.

THE RESPONSE

> Decide and display it in the King's Chambers.
> You are connected to the spirits.
> Cry out even if there is adversity.
> This information comes from the capital.
> It is not advantageous to approach people
> if you are armed.
> It is advantageous to have a direction to go.

Deciding and Parting describes your situation in terms of resolutely confronting difficulties. The way to deal with it is to clarify what you must do and announce it, even if you must leave something behind. You are facing a crisis and you must be honest about it. Bring out what is hidden. There is an angry old ghost in this situation, memories and experiences that have returned to take revenge on the living. Decide what to do. You have to tell your Friend about this, no matter what danger it may entail. You may have come to a parting of the ways. You have the strength, never fear. The spirits are with you. Don't be needlessly aggressive. Make your plans and act on them clearly and decisively. Break through the obstacles. The exposure to danger will only make you shine. Now is a time when the strong will endure. Bring your plans to completion.

SYMBOL, REFLECTION AND PRACTICE

Mists rise above Sky. Deciding and Parting. Inner struggle comes to expression through stimulating words. There is a source of great creative energy you can use.

Reflection: You have reached a decisive moment with each other. You may be facing the prospect of a major change in your relationship. Through this time, guide your actions by regularly contemplating the ultimate oneness of all things, even if separation is an issue. This prompts you to produce a replica of this oneness in your daily lives, which enables you more fully to come to terms with any deep rifts. Initially it may not seem that you know what is required, however, deep inside you, you do know. Make plain your intentions with each other and seek mutuality in your decisions. Be honest. Press on with the process. Action and expression are necessary. At the same time, modulate your words to avoid provoking needless contention.

Practice: During regular quiet time, see yourself as you see your partner. Live this fully. Imagine that you both radiate love, creativity and nobility, and that you are acting with clarity, determination and finesse. Include in your fantasy that you are completely and confidently resolved with each other—whether together or separated. Do at least one thing a day to express this resolution.

Transforming Lines

INITIAL NINE
Invigorating the leading foot.
If you go on you will not succeed. A mistake.

If you try to take the lead in this relationship, you will most certainly fail. You simply aren't prepared for it yet. This is not the way to go about things. *Direction*: Don't be afraid to act alone. You are coupled to a creative force. Use it well.

NINE AT SECOND
Alarms and outcries.
Absolutely no rest at night. Stay armed.
Have no cares.

A tense and invigorating situation for your relationship, with things coming from all sides. Don't worry. Let past sorrows go. You will obtain what you want. This can renew the creative life of your relationship. *Direction*: Revolution and renewal. You will be coupled with a creative force. Use it well.

NINE AT THIRD
Invigorating the cheekbones.
The Way closes.
The Relating Person must decide again and again.
She goes on alone and meets the rain.
She is as indignant as if she were soiled.
This is not a mistake.

You are involved with cruel people intent on their mastery. This Way is closed. See this clearly and leave now. You will be caught in a flood of insults and abuse. This is not a mistake. Be very clear and leave now. *Direction*: Express your feelings. Find supportive friends. The situation is already changing.

NINE AT FOURTH

> Your sacrum without flesh,
> Moving your resting place, hauling along
> the goat on a leash.
> The cause for sorrow disappears.
> When you hear people's words, do not trust them.

You have been punished or hurt by your Friend and are isolated. You must move to a new location. Stay adaptable. Don't get caught up in negative emotions. Fear not. Your sorrows will soon disappear. Don't believe what people tell you right now, and keep your own speech guarded. *Direction*: Wait for the right moment. Turn conflict into creative tension. The situation is already changing.

NINE AT FIFTH

> Reeds and highland, deciding, deciding.
> Moving your center is not a mistake.

You have to choose between two alternatives. You must decide. Don't be afraid of radical change. There is a creative force at work. *Direction*: Invigorate your ruling idea. Be resolute. You are connected to a creative force. Use it well.

SIX ABOVE

> You do not cry out.
> If you carry on like this the Way will close.

If you and your Friend don't communicate about what you are doing, you will be cut off and isolated. Call out. Tell each other about it. Now. *Direction*: Take action. You are connected to a creative force. Use it well.

妒 ䷫ 44 Coupling KOU

Welcome, encounter, open yourself to;
intense contact; all forms of sexual intercourse;
act through the yin.

SETTING THE STAGE

After you break through there are meetings. Thus there comes the time of Coupling. Accept this. Do not fear. Coupling means meetings. The supple meets the strong.

OPENING THE FIELD

Couple, KOU: meet, encounter, open yourself to; find someone on your path; coupling of yin and yang; all forms of sexual intercourse; mating, magnetism, gravity; gripped, overcome by passion; favorable, fortuitous. The ideogram shows two people making love.

THE RESPONSE

> **Coupling, the woman invigorates things.**
> **Don't use grasping the woman.**

Coupling describes your relationship, and your part in it, in terms of opening yourself to what comes. The way to deal with it is to realize that the brief and intense encounter contains great creative power. Don't try to control it. This passionate, fated encounter grips you with an overwhelming force. Yield to it. Welcome it. Open yourself to all that is new. But don't try to hold on. Yield and work through the feminine. Try to understand this supple strength. This is a time of brief, intense encounters that are full of a great creative power. Great events are moving here. These wonderful meetings come and go, like Heaven and Earth when they meet in a radiant moment. Don't try to cling and hang on. Your encounter will connect you with a creative force. Use it well.

SYMBOL, REFLECTION AND PRACTICE

Wind below Heaven. Coupling. The primal forces begin a new generation, as yin returns within. There is great creative energy available.

Reflection: Embrace the creative power of the times. Exchange passionately with your Friend. Regularly imagine this as a beautiful dance in which you both engage. Your dance is lyrical, captivating, loving, elegant and powerfully feminine. Others join you at every opportunity. The Way is through the yin with both men and women engaging through their femininity. Saturate each other with the primal energies you express in this way.

Practice: Meditate daily on how physical coupling is the expression in the world of spiritual oneness. Deliberately open to this divine union as fully as you can. Do things each day that promote joining and oneness between everyone and every thing.

Transforming Lines

INITIAL SIX

> **Attach it to a metal chock.**
> **Divination: the Way is open.**
> **If you have a direction to go, the Way will close.**
> **This is like an entangled pig with an injured hoof.**
> **There is a connection to the spirits.**

The Way is open and the two of you are connected to the spirit. But something is interfering with the flow of blessing. Give up your immediate plans and sort this out. If you try to control things, you'll get all tangled up. *Direction*: Take action. You are connected to a creative force. Use it well.

NINE AT SECOND
> **Enwrapped with fish inside.**
> **This is not a mistake.**
> **Hospitality is not advantageous.**

Stay quiet and withdrawn. Your ideas have born fruit and the womb is full. They need quiet and intimacy. It won't help you to be or receive a guest. *Direction*: Retreat and nourish the growing creative force. Use it well.

NINE AT THIRD
> **Your sacrum without flesh.**
> **You are moving your resting place.**
> **Adversity.**
> **Without the Great, you will make a mistake.**

You are isolated and have been punished or hurt by this relationship. Move to a new place. You will have to confront your past, but don't give in! You must find and believe in your central idea. *Direction*: Don't get involved in quarrels and wrangles. Find supportive friends. Gather energy for a decisive new move.

NINE AT FOURTH
> **Enwrapped with no fish inside.**
> **Rising up closes the Way.**

There are no creative possibilities in this relationship at the moment. Objecting or rebelling won't help. *Direction*: Gently penetrate to the core of the problem. Turn conflict into creative tension. The situation is already changing.

NINE AT FIFTH
> **Using osier to wrap the melons.**
> **A containing elegance tumbles down from Heaven.**

This is a beautiful inspiration. It is literally made in Heaven. What you do now will add elegance and beauty to all your life and your relationship. *Direction*: The founding of a noble line. Be resolute. You are connected to a creative force. Use it well.

NINE ABOVE

> **Coupling with your horns.**
> **Distress and confusion.**
> **This is not a mistake.**

You have turned a joyous experience into a trial of strength and sexual prowess. This is not a serious mistake, but it does leave you quite confused about what the relationship is all about. *Direction*: Don't be afraid to act alone. You are coupled with a creative force. Use it well.

萆 ䷬ 45 *Clustering* TS'UI

Gather, assemble, bunch together, collect; crowds; a great effort brings a great reward.

SETTING THE STAGE
Beings meet, then they will assemble. Thus there comes the time of Clustering. Accept this. Do not fear. Clustering means assembling.

OPENING THE FIELD
Cluster, TS'UI: gather or call together; groups of people or things; assemble, concentrate, collect; reunite; crowd, multitude; literally, dense clumps of grass. The ideogram suggests gathering the capacity to do things.

THE RESPONSE

Clustering will give you Success.
The King approaches the ancestral temple
to receive blessings for all.
Advantageous to see the Great Person. Success.
This is an Advantageous Divination.
Make a Great sacrifice. The Way is open.
It is advantageous to have a place to go.

Clustering describes your relationship, and your part in it, in terms of gathering and collecting energy. The way to deal with it is to unite both people and things through a common effort. This is a time for great projects. Do things together and with others. Assemble your resources and knowledge. See someone who can help you understand what is truly at stake. This is not just private emotion. Great ideas are needed as well as a great sacrifice. Make a plan and carry it out. Anticipate dangers so you are not taken by surprise. There is a great and joyous connection inherent in this time. Yield and work with it together.

SYMBOL, REFLECTION AND PRACTICE

Mist rises over the Earth. Clustering. An inner willingness to serve stimulates and brings people together. You can gradually advance to your goal.

Reflection: Take time to discuss your reasons for getting together with each other in the first place. Talk about your reasons for staying together. Realign yourselves, if necessary, so your goals are mutually held again. You need to move things forward and may need to get others involved. Your central purpose for being together can provide the necessary power around which all involved with you can align. In whatever you do, act together. Share your goals and ensure that they support the welfare of all concerned. You can be adventurous. All the same, remain sensibly alert to possible difficulties.

Practice: Imagine everyone involved is collected together. You imagine them surrounded by a beautiful energy that harmonizes and floods them with light. All becomes clear and aligned by this energy. The way ahead gradually becomes obvious. Keep doing this repeatedly, until it is.

Transforming Lines

INITIAL SIX
There is a connection to the spirits that is not complete.
Thus there is now disorder, now Clustering.
Like an outcry, one grasp of the hand brings laughter.
Have no cares. Going on is not a mistake.

Your relationship is connected to a deep source of energy, but the link is unclear. That is why things are so uneven, one moment joyous, the next moment confused. Don't worry. Reach out and touch each other and the tension dissolves into laughter and joy. This is certainly not a mistake. The connection is real. *Direction*: Follow this stream of events. Proceed step by step. Gather energy for a decisive new move.

Six at Second

> **Draw things out, this opens the Way.**
> **There is a connection to the spirit.**
> **It is advantageous to make dedications.**

The energy for the relationship is there, but it is going to take a while to emerge. Don't be in a hurry. Draw things out. That will open the Way. Make an offering of the things you believe in, even if your resources are slim. *Direction*: Look within to find the way out. Find supportive friends. Gather energy for a decisive new move.

Six at Third

> **First Clustering, then lamenting.**
> **No direction is advantageous.**
> **Going on is not a mistake.**
> **Being Small now will bring distress and confusion.**

As soon as you begin to make changes in your relationship, you are swamped by a flood of sorrow and painful memories. There is really nothing you can do here. Leave gently and quietly. It is not a mistake. If you simply try to adapt to the situation, you will be covered in distress and confusion. *Direction*: Be open to a new influence. It will couple you with a creative force. Use it well.

Nine at Fourth

> **The Great Way opens. This is not a mistake.**

You can do anything you want to do now in this relationship if you act with a full and loving heart. The Great Way is open.

Nothing you do would be a mistake. *Direction*: Change your group. Strip away old ideas. Be open and provide what is needed.

NINE AT FIFTH

Clustering in rank.
This is not a mistake. No need to sacrifice.
Divination: an ever-flowing source.
The cause of sorrow will disappear.

This is a friendly, honest relationship that can be a long-term source of comfort and inspiration. Keep working. The doubt and sorrow you feel will disappear and the relationship will be grounded. *Direction*: Gather energy in order to act when the call comes. Re-imagine the situation. Gather energy for a decisive new move.

SIX ABOVE

Paying tribute with sighs, tears and moans.
This is not your mistake.

This is a difficult connection. You pay for it with your tears. Though nothing here is really your fault, are you sure you want to endure this? *Direction*: Communication is obstructed. Proceed step by step. Gather energy for a decisive new move.

升 ䷭ 46 Ascending SHENG

Make the effort, don't worry; climb the mountain step by step; lift yourself, fulfill the potential; advance, rise.

SETTING THE STAGE
Assembling with what is above means that this situation is called Ascending. Accept this. Do not fear. Ascending means things don't simply come to you.

OPENING THE FIELD
Ascend, SHENG: mount, go up, rise; climb step by step, advance through your own efforts; be promoted, rise in office; accumulate, fulfill the potential; distill liquor. Literally, a Small measure.

THE RESPONSE
> **Ascending will give you Fundamental Success.**
> **Use and see the Great Person.**
> **Have no cares.**
> **Chastising in the south opens the Way.**

Ascending describes your relationship, or your part in it, in terms of rising to a higher level and greater connection. The way to deal with it is to set a goal and work toward it step by step. Root yourselves and push toward the heights. In the end, this will bring you exactly what you want. Put yourself in order. See people who can help you. See what is great in your love and your life. The Way to the source of energy is open here. This generates meaning and good fortune by releasing transformative energy. You are undoubtedly on your way. It is time to put the chaos of your lives behind you. Work hard to realize this. Correct things and set out together. Your purpose is already moving.

SYMBOL, REFLECTION AND PRACTICE

Earth center gives birth to the Trees. Ascending. Inner penetration ascends the outer field of action. You can realize hidden potential.

Reflection: Figure out what you want with each other. Systematically set out to achieve these things, one small step at a time. Persist in doing whatever is necessary. Get together every day to review your progress and to plan your next steps. These meetings are crucial for staying sensitive to your shared inner guidance, your concerns and your hopes. Open yourselves up to each other and share what you each know is fundamentally important. Make sure you do something every day to achieve your overall goals, even if what you do is seemingly insignificant.

Practice: Regularly concentrate on how to align with the Way. Seek inner guidance by asking for it from Heaven. Keep your overall direction clear in this way. Do at least three things a day, no matter how small, that will help realize your alignment.

Transforming Lines

INITIAL SIX
Sincere ascending. The Great Way opens.

You have been recognized. Your Friend has become aware of your value. Now all the doors are open to you. Climb the mountain and find what you desire. *Direction*: A great and flourishing time begins. If you let yourself be led, you can realize hidden potential. The situation is already changing.

NINE AT SECOND
**There is a connection to the spirits,
It is advantageous to make dedications.**

The connection between you is established. Dedicate yourself to what you believe in together. It is all there if you want it to be. *Direction*: Stay simple and connected to the facts. Release bound energy. The situation is already changing.

NINE AT THIRD
> You ascend into an empty city.

There is no resistance to you now. This is not a place to doubt. Don't stop, push on. *Direction*: Organize your forces. Something significant is returning. Be open and provide what is needed.

SIX AT FOURTH
> The King makes a sacrifice
> And receives blessing on the Twin-peaked Mountain.
> The Way is open. This is not a mistake.

You have found a powerful place in the life of this relationship and the family around it. Dedicate your efforts to the common good. The Way is open. This is not a mistake. *Direction*: Continue in your path. Be resolute. You are connected to a creative force. Use it well.

SIX AT FIFTH
> Divination: the Way is open.
> Ascend the steps.

There are no barriers to your progress and your relationship. Proceed step by step. The Way is open to you. *Direction*: Connect to common needs and strengths. Be resolute. You are connected to a creative force. Use it well.

SIX ABOVE
> Ascending in dim light.
> Divination: it is advantageous not to pause.

You are climbing in the dark. You can't really see where this relationship is going. Don't stop now. Pushing on will bring both profit and insight in the end. *Direction*: Renovate a corrupt situation. If you let yourself be led, you can realize hidden potential. The situation is already changing.

困 ☰☷ 47 Confining/ Oppression K'UN

Oppressed, restricted, exhausted, cut off; at the end of your resources; the moment of truth; search within to find the way out.

SETTING THE STAGE

Ascending without end will eventually confine you. Thus there comes the time of Confining. Accept this. Do not fear. Confining will mean mutual meetings.

OPENING THE FIELD

Confine, K'UN: enclosed, restricted, persecuted; punishment, penal codes, prison; worry, fear, anxiety; fatigue, exhausted, at the end of your resources; disheartened, weary, afflicted; poor; The ideogram shows a growing tree in an enclosure.

THE RESPONSE

Confining will give you Success.
Divination: the Great Person opens the Way.
When you hear words, don't trust them.

Confining describes your situation in terms of being cut off, oppressed and exhausted. The way to deal with it is to collect the energy to break out of the enclosure and re-establish communication. This is a truly oppressive situation, either as a couple or as an individual. It cuts you off from what you need. Gather your strength within and, above all, wait for the right moment to move. Talk to people who can help you see the situation. Learn to see the great in yourself or your relationship. If you have supportive friends, stay in touch with them. This generates meaning and good fortune by releasing transforma-tive energy. Don't get caught up in the expression of negative emotions. The purpose of this limitation is not to make you suffer, but to force you to find your own connection to what is real. There is a mandate for change hidden here that can show your purpose. Correct your own thinking and find out where you are deluding yourself.

SYMBOL, REFLECTION AND PRACTICE

Mists without Stream. Confining. Stimulation and contact are drawn into the inner stream, cutting off the possibility of communication. You will find the people you want to live with.

Reflection: You each need to go deeply inside. Work out what is going on and get very clear on this. This is not a time for trying to talk or act things out. You have resources deep within you. Take the time each day to go inside and find them. When you do, you will recharge and strengthen yourself. Do this by sitting quietly and locating yourself in that part of you from which you notice everything inside and outside, the "I" inside you. In this position, experience fully whatever is in your awareness. This will take you on a kind of ride through experiences as one fol-lows another. Regularly pay attention to the physical world around you so you stay balanced through this process. During your day-to-day life, find support with friends, let go of grudges and clear yourself in readiness for the change that going inside will bring.

Practice: Go inside regularly and call on help from Heaven. Ask for guidance and support about what to do. Imagine that what you need is energy that showers all around and through you. As it does, it heals, frees, corrects and guides everyone. Stay alert for changes to show in your daily life.

Transforming Lines

INITIAL SIX
> Confined, punished with a wooden rod.
> If you enter this shadowy gully,
> You will encounter no one for three years.

You have been hurt or punished by your Friend, but you are your own worst enemy now. Do not retreat into melancholy and dark pleasures. You will completely cut yourself off. *Direction*: Express yourself. Find supportive friends. Gather energy for a decisive new move.

NINE AT SECOND
> Confined at eating and drinking.
> Scarlet sashes are coming on all sides.
> It is advantageous to make presentations and oblations.
> Chastising closes the Way. This is not a mistake.

You ostensibly have all you need. But your Friend does not recognize the importance of the relationship. Don't worry, that recognition is coming. It will change the whole way you see yourself and your relationship. Offer a sacrifice now to the things you believe in. Don't try to make others take the blame for your situation. This is not a mistake. *Direction*: Gather resources for a great new project. Proceed step by step. Gather energy for a decisive new move.

SIX AT THIRD
> Confined by stones. Grasping thorns.
> You enter your palace. You do not see your consort.
> The Way closes.

You don't need anyone else to oppress you. You do it very well yourself at the moment. You beat yourself against impossible obstacles and grasp at things that hurt you. You can't even see your Friend, who loves you and is eager to support you. This kind of behavior will get you absolutely nowhere. *Direction*: A time of transition. Don't be afraid to act alone. You are connected to a creative force. Use it well.

NINE AT FOURTH

> **It comes slowly, slowly, confined in a metal chariot.**
> **Distress and confusion, but it ends well.**

The solution to your emotional problems will arrive very slowly. This is partially because you are bound up in old thoughts and dreams of gain. It will take a change of heart to recognize the truth of your relationship. This will turn out well for all in the end. *Direction*: When the right moment comes, take the risk. Take things in. Be open and provide what is needed.

NINE AT FIFTH

> **Nose cutting and foot cutting,**
> **Oppressed by the men in crimson sashes.**
> **Slowly this will be loosened.**
> **It is advantageous to offer oblations.**

You are punished and oppressed by a misguided sense of authority in this relationship. This is serious, but the bitter feelings will slowly loosen and you will be set free. Until this day comes, make offerings to your ideals. What your heart feels deeply will help you through. *Direction*: Release bound energy. The situation is already changing.

SIX ABOVE

> **Confined by trailing creepers, unsteady and unsettled.**
> **Say it like this: "If you stir up the causes of sorrow,**
> **there will be sorrowing."**
> **Chastising opens the Way.**

Stop indulging yourself! This shouldn't even bother you. If you sit around and groan about your relationship all the time, all you will hear is lamentation. Take yourself in hand. Get yourself in order. That will open the Way. Don't just sit around trying to make everyone feel guilty. *Direction*: Don't get involved in quarrels or wrangles. Find supportive friends. Gather energy for a decisive new move.

井 ䷯ 48 *The Well* CHING

**Communicate, interact; the underlying structure, the
network; source of life-water needed by all.**

SETTING THE STAGE

If you are confined by what is above, the situation will reverse
itself below. Thus there comes the time of The Well. Accept this.
Do not fear. The Well means interpenetrating.

OPENING THE FIELD

Well, CHING: water well, well at the center of a group of nine
fields; resources held in common; underlying structure, be in
good order, regular; communicate with others, common needs;
the water of life, the inner source. The ideogram shows a group
of nine fields with the well at the center.

THE RESPONSE

> **The Well. Alter the city, but you cannot alter the well.**
> **Without loss, without gain, going and coming,**
> **The well is always the well.**
> **A muddy bottom, no rope in the well**
> **or ruining the pitcher:**
> **These things will close the Way.**

The Well describes your relationship, or your part in it, in terms
of an underlying structure and the natural force that flows in it.
The way to deal with it is to clarify and renew your connection
to this source. Recognize the deep needs we all feel and find the
sources of life that are there for us to draw on. Without this, your
relationship will wither. You can change your clothes or the city
you live in, but the well and the common human needs and
strengths it represents will never change. The well shows you

how to communicate by recognizing your common humanity. Make contact with this deep source of life. If you let the life-water turn to mud, if you can't reach far enough or if you ruin the container that holds it, then the Way to the water will close. You will be cut off from those you love. The Well can free you both from isolation. It means communication and interconnection. Stay where you are and work for what is best in you and your relationship. This well will nourish you without ever being exhausted.

SYMBOL, REFLECTION AND PRACTICE

Stream above Wood. The Well. The water of life wells up from the deep inner ground. You can turn discord into creative tension.

Reflection: When centered in the affection or love that you experience with your Friend, regularly bring others into your awareness so they are bathed in your love too. Together you create a combined center which is a primary source of life. You nourish each other with this life and you nourish others. Make sure that you take care of your shared center so its life-giving sustenance is always abundant. Pay attention, too, to your connections with others. Ensure that you remain available, and that you don't become unavailable to them through neglecting or abusing your contacts with them. Your mutual health and strength depends on sharing with each other. It also depends on sharing what you have with others.

Practice: Cultivate love at all times. To do this, put your hand or hands over your heart and imagine that a little replica of you is seated happily in your heart. Notice the warmth, soft light and mellow sounds of the love in your heart. With others, share what you have and who you are, at least in small ways, as a natural expression of love. Seek unity and alignment with all.

Transforming Lines

INITIAL SIX
> This well is a bog, no one can drink the water.
> It is an ancient well that no birds come to.

The sources of your relationship are muddy and bogged down. Nothing good will come of doing things this way. It is time to change. *Direction*: Wait for the right moment to act. Turn conflict into creative tension. You can realize hidden potential. The situation is already changing.

NINE AT SECOND
> This well is a gully where people shoot fish in pairs.
> The jug is cracked and leaking.

The sources of this relationship are not taken care of. Each seeks their own gain. There is no container. Time to change. *Direction*: Re-imagine the situation.

NINE AT THIRD
> This well is unsettled and the water is not drunk.
> "This makes my heart ache."
> Its water could be drawn if the King
> were bright-minded.
> We could accept this blessing together.

This is the sorrow of someone who has much to give, but no one to give it to. There is nothing you can do. Move on and have no fear. In the end you will be recognized. *Direction*: Take the risk. Be open and provide what is needed.

SIX AT FOURTH
> This well is being lined.

A time of inner work and improvement. You may feel cut off from your Friend, but have no fears. This inner work is not a mistake. *Direction*: A time of transition. Don't be afraid to act alone. You are connected to a creative force. Use it well.

NINE AT FIFTH
This well has cold, clear spring water to drink.

This relationship is a clear, pure source of life-water for everyone to draw on. Use it and give thanks. *Direction*: Make the effort. If you let yourself be led, you can realize your hidden potential. The situation is already changing.

SIX ABOVE
This well collects all without a cover.
There is a connection to the spirits.
The Way to the Source is open.

Receive and give things freely. Your relationship is a source of spiritual nourishment for everyone. Don't hide it away. The Way is fundamentally open. You can accomplish great things together. *Direction*: Gently penetrate to the heart of things. Turn conflict into creative tension. The situation is already changing.

革 ☰ 49 *Skinning/ Revolution* KO

Strip away the old; let the new life emerge; revolt and renew; molting.

SETTING THE STAGE

The Way of the Well does not allow you not to Skin things. Thus there comes the time of Skinning. Accept this. Do not fear. Skinning means previous sorrows are left behind.

OPENING THE FIELD

Skinning, KO: take off the skin, shed skin, molt; radical change, renew, revolt, overthrow, revolution; skin, leather armor, soldiers; eliminate, repeal, cut off, cut away. The ideogram shows a skin stretched on a frame.

THE RESPONSE

**Skinning. On your own day
There will be a connection to the spirits.
Fundamental Success: Advantageous Divination.
The cause for sorrow disappears.**

Skinning describes your relationship, or your part in it, in terms of stripping away the cover so new life within can emerge. The way to deal with it is to help this new life to radically change how things are presented. You must change how you act together. It isn't working now. It is covered over with old habits, false goals and oppressive rules. It is time that the snake shed its skin. Strip away the old. Eliminate what has become useless. Throw out the decadent and corrupt. Act with confidence. This will begin a whole new cycle of time, full of success, profit and insight. Forget about old quarrels. Present yourselves in a brand new way. The mandate from Heaven is changing. Yield to it and serve the emergence of the new. Your doubts and sorrows will be extinguished.

Symbol, Reflection and Practice

Fire in the Mists. Skinning. Changing awareness strips away the obsolete to reveal a stimulating new potential. A passionate connection. You can realize your hidden potential.

Reflection: Singly and together, an important question needs to be asked at this time about everything: "How does what I am thinking, feeling and doing support our friendship?" Anything that does not, needs to be discarded or changed. This is time to shed the old and reveal the new. It is very easy to develop habits when living with others. These need to go. It is time to review everything again. As you do, show your true self to your Friend. Take the risk. What is under the surface is beautiful. Share who you are confidently.

Practice: Every day open your eyes to the new sun and the new day. Affirm this as a new beginning for everything. Cultivate a sense of wonder at the newness of everything. Ask: "Who am I?" "Who are you?"

Transforming Lines

Initial Nine
Tightly secured in yellow cowhide.

Nothing can tear you away from this relationship. You can't do anything to change things now, but be open to the impulse when it comes. *Direction*: Don't be afraid to act alone. You are coupled to a creative force. Use it well.

SIX AT SECOND
> **This is your own day, so skin it!**
> **Chastising opens the Way. This is not a mistake.**

This is your time. You can change the world. Put your relationship in order. Don't be shy. Be a hero. Vigorous action opens the Way. This is definitely not a mistake. *Direction*: Be resolute. You are connected to a creative force. Use it well.

NINE AT THIRD
> **Chastising closes the Way. Divination: adversity.**
> **When the renewing words draw near three times,**
> **You will be connected to the spirits.**

Discipline and expeditions won't work now. There is danger for the relationship from the past. Let the call to action go around three times, then act decisively. You can renew the time. The spirits will help you. *Direction*: Follow the stream of events. Proceed step by step. Gather energy for a decisive new move.

NINE AT FOURTH
> **The cause for sorrow disappears.**
> **There is a connection to the spirits.**
> **Change Heaven's mandates.**
> **The Way is open.**

Act and have no doubts. All your sorrows will vanish. The spirits are helping you. You are in a position to change the imaginative basis of your relationship. The Way is open. *Direction*: The situation is already changing.

NINE AT FIFTH
> **The Great Person transforms like a tiger.**
> **Even before the auguries he is connected to the spirits.**

When the time comes to change, your relationship must change with it. Let your great creative strength be seen. Pursue what you desire. Even before there is an oracle, people will know you are connected to the spirits. Have no fear. Your inner pattern can brighten events. *Direction*: A time of great abundance. Don't be afraid to act alone. You are connected to a creative force. Use it well.

Six Above

> The Relating Person transforms like a leopard,
> While Small People can only skin their face.
> Chastising closes the Way.
> Stay where you are now. Divination:
> the Way is open.

Change your relationship with grace and elegance. Most people just change their face, but you must go deeper than that. Don't try to discipline the people around you. Stay right where you are for now, and the changes will fall into your hands. *Direction*: Give people a common purpose. This will couple you with a creative force. Use it well.

鼎 ䷱ *50 The Vessel* TING

Sacred vessel; hold, contain and transform, imagine; meal with spirits, ancestors and noble people; establish, found.

SETTING THE STAGE

Skinning things means you must have a Vessel in which to transform them. Thus there comes the time of the Vessel. Accept this. Do not fear. The Vessel means grasping renewal.

OPENING THE FIELD

Vessel, TING: cast bronze cauldron with three feet and two ears, a sacred vessel for cooking offerings and ritual meals; symbol of a family or dynasty; hold, contain, transform, transmute; connect with the spirits; establish, secure, foundation; precious. The ancient ideogram shows questioning the spirits.

THE RESPONSE

**The Vessel. The Way to the Source is open.
Success.**

The Vessel describes your relationship, and your part in it, in terms of sacrifice, imagination and the spiritual capacity of a sacred vessel. The way to deal with it is to contain and transform your relationship through the power of a symbol that can move your heart. You need to see deeply into your problems, to examine and reflect until their meaning emerges. Ground your work in the world of the spirit. The everyday events of your life must be transmuted into symbolic images. Then they become a vessel of transformation that connects both of you to the invisible powers that surround us. Break through your old habits. By using the vessel you can experience renewal. The vessel means using symbols to transform your relationship and becoming aware of their power. This brightens your understanding. Security and a new beginning will come from this. It generates meaning and good fortune by releasing transformative energy.

SYMBOL, REFLECTION AND PRACTICE
Fire above Wood. Vessel. Inner penetration feeds and spreads the growing light of awareness. You can act clearly and decisively.

Reflection: Your relationship can help you become one with spirit. Its transforming power comes from your unique reasons for getting together. Everything each of you needs to do for this oneness is within what you have with each other. The way to do it is to become one, to transform two to one. Do this by claiming all aspects of your Friend as your own, whatever they are. Imagine that you have taken on all that he or she is. While doing this, accept whatever you experience. Keep yourself linked to the physical world. It will help your system to digest and manage what you experience. Only what is real and can endure will be strengthened. The rest will dissolve away. By unifying yourself in this way, you become more at one with each other. Your direct experience of Heaven arises as you progressively realize this oneness.

Practice: To balance your yin and yang energy, take time each day to contemplate the balance in you. As a woman, meditate your body as a man's. As a man, meditate your body as a woman's. Understand that the transformation completes your energetic balance and helps to make you whole.

Transforming Lines

INITIAL SIX
The Vessel toppled over by the foot.
Advantageous: the obstruction comes out.
This is like acquiring a concubine for the sake of a son.
This is not a mistake.

Do something out of the ordinary in this relationship to establish a connection with the spirit world. Turn things on their head. Get rid of the obstruction. This is not a mistake. It will bring you happiness. *Direction*: A great and flourishing time is coming. Be resolute. You are connected to a creative force. Use it well.

NINE AT SECOND

There is something real in the Vessel.
My companion is afflicted but cannot approach me.
The Way is open.

You have something real going on inside you, a spiritual transformation. Your Friend is afflicted with negative emotions. Stay with the transformation. Don't fear. It is substantial and secure. The Way is open. Proceed on your own. *Direction*: Search outside the norms. Don't be afraid to act alone. You are connected to a creative force. Use it well.

NINE AT THIRD

The Vessel's ears are skinned.
Movement is hindered.
The pheasant juice is not eaten.
Rain comes on all sides and lessens the cause of sorrow.
Bringing this to completion opens the Way.

Everything in the relationship feels clogged up now. Don't worry about it. This is a transformation of the way the two of you understand things. The rain will come and wash away your sorrows. Keep going. The Way is open. *Direction*: Gather energy for a decisive new move.

NINE AT FOURTH

The Vessel's stand is severed.
The Prince's meal is overthrown and his form is soiled.
The Way closes.

Disaster. Whatever you are contemplating, don't do it. You will betray a trust. The Way is closed. *Direction*: Renovate a corrupt situation. If you let yourself be led, you can realize hidden potential. The situation is already changing.

Six at Fifth

> **The Vessel has yellow ears and metal rings.**
> **Advantageous Divination.**

A beautiful vision and a loving plan. You have found a way to bring this relationship into the world. This is a great joy. Act on it. It will bring you profit and insight. *Direction*: This couples you with a creative force. Use it well.

Nine Above

> **The Vessel has jade rings.**
> **The Great Way opens.**
> **There is nothing that is not advantageous.**

This relationship is truly precious. It can transform your lives. The Great Way is open to you now. This can be of benefit to all. It will open a whole new world. *Direction*: Continue on. Be resolute. You are connected with a creative force. Use it well.

震 ䷲ *51 Shake* CHEN

Disturbing and fertilizing shock; sexual energy; wake up, stir up; return of life in early spring.

SETTING THE STAGE
The Lord's implements need the powerful Elder Son to use them. Thus there comes the time of Shake. Accept this. Do not fear. Shake means stirring things up. Shake means rising up.

OPENING THE FIELD
Shake, CHEN: arouse, inspire, wake up, begin, set in motion; shock, frighten, awe, alarm; sexual arousal; thunder (comes from below in Chinese thought), earthquake; terrify, trembling, severe; excite, influence, action; break through the shell, come out of the bud. The ideogram shows rain and the sign for exciting.

Shake is one of the Eight Helping Spirits. Shake is the Arouser and Exorcist, driving out the old, rousing and opening the field of the new. He is flamboyant and sexual, luxuriating, frightening and inspiriting, green and full of juice. He is in motion and moves all things. He is an emerging dragon.

THE RESPONSE
Shake will give you Success.
Shake comes, frightening, frightening!
Then laughing words, shouting, shouting!
Though Shake scares people for a hundred miles
when he appears,
But you do not spill the Ladle and Libation.

Shake describes your relationship, or your part in it, in terms of a disturbing and inspiring shock. The way to deal with it is to vigorously rouse things to new activity. The new energy is frightening at first, for it challenges all the boundaries. It is like a new spring, a chance to start over. Don't lose the chance to work with it. Rouse things up to new activity. Re-imagine your situation. The moment when the thunder returns to begin the year is a gift of the spirits.

This is a pivoting phase, where change can occur quickly and fundamentally. If you want to alter your relationship, apply yourself now.

SYMBOL, REFLECTION AND PRACTICE

Reiterating Thunder. Powerful energy thrusts up from below, stirring everything to new growth. You can re-imagine a difficult situation.

Reflection: Good will come from the disturbance you are experiencing. Embrace it as a creative force for change, an opportunity to change fundamentally and to reconnect deeply and lovingly. Imagine that you have acted in the same way as your Friend in whatever is disturbing you and stirring things up. Include what you like as well as anything you are not happy with. Accepting these experiences in yourself is a prelude to accepting them in others. Your acceptance can help you to let go of what you are holding onto. Then you can join with each other with new understanding and union. Affection and love always expand with greater union. A new season is dawning.

Practice: Take time each day to contemplate what is happening now. Look for the causes of challenging feelings. As you do, realize that they arise because of limited perception. Accept the feelings. Expand your views, soften your body, open your heart, accept the unacceptable, join the irreconcilable, and include it with tenderness. Watch it dissolve into new awareness.

Transforming Lines

INITIAL NINE
> **Shake comes, frightening, frightening.**
> **Then laughing words, shouting, shouting.**
> **The Way is open.**

A profound shock that you both experience. Everything is turned
upside down. But the anxiety soon turns to joy and a burst of
creative energy. Let it move you. The Way is open. *Direction*:
Gather resources in order to act when the call comes. Re-imagine
the situation. Gather energy for a decisive new move.

SIX AT SECOND
> **Shake comes and brings adversity.**
> **Your hundred thousand coins are lost.**
> **Climb the Ninth Mountain.**
> **Don't pursue what has been lost.**
> **On the seventh day you will acquire it again.**

You think you have lost something precious. Don't grieve. Climb
the mound of transformation. Everything you lost will soon
return. *Direction*: If you let yourself be led, you can realize hidden
potential. The situation is already changing.

SIX AT THIRD
> **Shake reviving, reviving!**
> **Shake moves without mistakes.**

This shock rouses your dormant creative energy. The relationship
is renewed and inspired. Move with it. You will not be making a
mistake. *Direction*: A time of abundance is coming. Don't be
afraid to act alone. You are connected to a creative force. Use it
well.

NINE AT FOURTH
Shake released from a bog.

This fertile energy releases you from a cloud of confusion. The relationship has been bogged down. What happened? Try to understand where it came from. *Direction:* Something significant is returning. Be open and provide what is needed.

SIX AT FIFTH
Shake comes and goes. Adversity.
Don't lose your purpose. There will be things to do.

The creative energy comes and goes. It brings up old memories and quarrels and you must deal with them together. Keep your mind on what you want to do. You will have plenty to keep you busy. *Direction:* Follow the stream of events. Proceed step by step. Gather energy for a decisive new move.

SIX ABOVE
Shake, twisting, twisting.
Observing it you are terrified, terrified.
Chastising closes the Way.
The shake is not in your body,
but in your neighbor's body.
Be calm. This is not a mistake.
There will be words about a marriage.

Creative energy twists and turns, driving people around the two of you into a frenzy. Do not worry about this. Stay calm and stay together. Don't get caught in the trap. *Direction:* Bite through the obstacles. Re-imagine the situation. Gather energy for a decisive new move.

艮 ☶ *52 Bound/Stabilize*
KEN

Calm, still, stabilize; bind, come to the limit or boundary; articulating your experiences; becoming individual.

SETTING THE STAGE
Beings cannot always be aroused, so now they are stilled. Thus there comes the time of Bound. Accept this. Do not fear. Bound means stilling things.

OPENING THE FIELD
Bound, KEN: limit, boundary, obstacle; still, quiet, calm, stable, tranquil; enclose, mark off, confine, stabilize; finish, bring to an end; reflect on the past; simple, clear, straightforward; the mountain as a refuge and a barrier; stop, bring to a standstill. The ideogram shows someone turning around to look at the past.
Bound is one of the Eight Helping Spirits. His words bind us and accomplish fate. Bound leads through perceiving and fixing limits. He is nemesis. He articulates fate. He is the still point in all turning, the refuge of distant mountains. He is a dog, guarding, watching and finding.

THE RESPONSE

Binding your back,
Stilling desires so they do not catch on things,
Move through your chambers without
seeing your people.
This is not a mistake.

Bound describes your relationship, or your place in it, in terms of recognizing a limit and coming to the end of a cycle. The way to deal with it is to calm and stabilize your emotions and desires in order to articulate what has been accomplished, for in it you will find the seed of the new. Look at what you have done and what has held you together and what problems you have faced so that you can see where to go next. Still your immediate emotional responses so things can not carry you away. See through your desires. Calm yourselves and give voice to your experiences and your insight. This is not a mistake. Bound can give you the chance to look very deeply into things, to their hidden sources. It can stabilize and articulate your love.

> This is a pivoting phase, where change can occur quickly and fundamentally. If you want to alter your relationship, apply yourself now.

Symbol, Reflection and Practice

Joining Mountains. Bound. Accomplishing words articulate the past and suggest the new. You can be delivered from tension and suffering.

Reflection: Take time to sit together doing nothing. You are at the end of a phase in your time as Friends. Allow time for this completion to express itself fully. Just because you have been active, you don't need to stay active. Keep still and wait for what comes next. Encourage calm and quietness with each other. What you have created is the foundation of what comes next. Like the in-breath following the out-breath, or the reverse, accept the transition between the two with equanimity. Your new flow will arise in its own time.

Practice: Sit and breathe. Notice how your have to breathe in so you can breathe out, and you have to breathe out so you can breathe in. Relax at the transitions between the two and allow the transition to extend itself for as long as it naturally does. Avoid holding your breath. Relax and let the moment extend if it does.

Transforming Lines

INITIAL SIX

Binding your feet.
This is not a mistake
Divination: this will be perpetually advantageous.

When an impulse to action comes, try to hold back before it leads you into all sorts of compulsive entanglements. This is not a mistake. It can change your relationship for the better. *Direction*: Beautify things. Release tensions. The situation is already changing.

SIX AT SECOND

Your calves are bound.
You can't rescue your following.
"My heart is not glad."

You stop running after impossible desires, but you cannot help your Friend, who is on the same course. This is what makes your heart ache. *Direction*: Renovate a corrupt situation. If you let yourself be led, you can realize hidden potential. The situation is already changing.

NINE AT THIRD

You bind yourself by assigning restraints
to your loins.
Adversity smothers your heart.

You are cutting yourself off from your real desire. The acrid smoke smothers your heart. You don't have to suffer like this. It won't help your Friend and it won't help the relationship. *Direction*: Strip away old ideas. Be open and provide what is needed.

Six at Fourth

> **Binding your trunk, stilling your emotions.**
> **This is not a mistake.**

Still your compulsive actions and desires for now. This frees you from mistakes and lets you see where your real motivations lie. *Direction*: Search outside the norms. Don't be afraid to act alone. You are connected to a creative force. Use it well.

Six at Fifth

> **Your jaws are bound,**
> **So your words have order.**
> **The cause for sorrow disappears.**

If you reflect and restrain your speech, what you say will have order and elegance. When you can communicate to your Friend like this, your sorrows will vanish. *Direction*: Proceed step by step. Gather energy for a decisive new move.

Nine Above

> **Generosity at the boundary. The Way is open.**

Meet your Friend with generosity, honesty and care. This is the end of your isolation. You have learned what you need to face your new life together. The Way is open. Good luck. *Direction*: Release bound energy. The situation is already changing.

漸 ☴ 53 *Gradual Advance*
CHIEN

Smooth, adaptable progress; infiltrate, penetrate like water; ceremonies leading to a formal marriage.

SETTING THE STAGE

Nothing can be completely stilled. Thus there comes the time of Gradual Advance. Accept this. Do not fear. Gradual Advance means advancing. Gradual Advance means the marrying woman who waits for the man to move.

OPENING THE FIELD

Gradual Advance, CHIEN: Advance by degrees, gracefully; penetrate slowly and surely; adapt, infiltrate; flexible, supple, submissive; permeate, influence, affect; formal marriage and festivities of the eldest daughter. The ideogram shows water infiltrating through obstacles.

THE RESPONSE

Gradual Advance.
Act like a Marrying Woman. The Way is open.
Advantageous Divination.

Gradual Advance describes your relationship, or your part in it, in terms of gradually achieving a desired goal. It shows the ceremonies leading to a marriage. The way to deal with it is to advance slowly and surely through gentle penetration, permeating to the center of the situation like water. This generates meaning and good fortune by releasing transformative energy. You are slowly and surely moving toward union and the culmination. Deal with this situation through adaptability, subtle penetration and grace. Embrace the yin. Don't try to order people around. Wait for the proper signs and signals. This gentle penetration will bring you to the place where you belong. You don't have to force anything. The symbol of this situation is a pair of wild geese who go through all life's tribulations together.

Symbol, Reflection and Practice

Tree above Mountain. Gradual Advance. Inner stability lets you penetrate the outer world. You gather energy for an important new move.

Reflection: While waiting for the opportunities that are opening up to present themselves, keep imagining the outcome you desire as already completed. Make what you imagine open enough for events to unfold in ways that may pleasantly surprise you. Avoid blocking what you need by restricting the fantasy of what you want. Leave space for Heaven to surprise you. Imagine that everything has already worked out well. By practicing this approach, you can act with the gentle determination that your situation is calling for. You can trust that everything you need will be there for you at the right time. Do something simple each day to promote your goal.

Practice: Open yourself daily to the rhythm of life. Notice the way that momentum builds quickly once a pause is past. Look at the world around you: at the cycles of the sun and moon and the tides, at the waves breaking on the shore.

Transforming Lines

Initial Six

> The wild geese gradually advance to a barrier.
> The Small Son encounters adversity
> and there are words.
> This situation is not a mistake.

Together you encounter danger from the past, but the creative energy is still there. This is not a mistake. Have no fear. Speak out. *Direction*: Gather energy for a decisive new move.

SIX AT SECOND

> **The wild geese gradually advance to the stone.**
> **They eat and drink, feasting, feasting.**
> **The Way is open.**

A secure place and a warm connection. Enjoy your relationship now. The Way is open. The journey will resume. *Direction*: Gently penetrate to the heart of things. Turn conflict into creative tension. The situation is already changing.

NINE AT THIRD

> **The wild geese gradually advance to the highlands.**
> **The husband is on campaign and doesn't return.**
> **The wife is pregnant and doesn't nurture her child.**
> **The Way closes.**
> **It is advantageous to resist becoming an outlaw.**

You have taken a wrong turn. Things are falling apart in mutual recrimination. The Way is closing and the creative energy is dispersed. Firmly resist the temptation to become violent or withholding. Find what you can do to help each other. *Direction*: Let everything come into view. Strip away old ideas. Be open and provide what is needed.

SIX AT FOURTH

> **The wild geese gradually advance to the trees.**
> **Perhaps they acquire a flat branch to rest on,**
> **the rafter of a house.**
> **This is not a mistake.**

This is a resting place after a great transition. It will give your relationship shelter for a while. Have no fear, this is not a mistake. *Direction*: Through retiring you will be coupled with a creative force. Use it well.

NINE AT FIFTH

> The wild geese gradually advance to the
> grave mounds.
> The wife is not pregnant for three years.
> When this is complete, absolutely nothing
> can stop you.
> The Way is open.

This is the penultimate step, where the creative energy in this relationship makes contact with the ancestors and the guardian spirits. This takes time, but when it is finished nothing will stop you. Have no fears. The Way is open. *Direction*: Stabilize your desires. Release bound energy. The situation is already changing.

NINE ABOVE

> The wild geese gradually advance to the highlands.
> Their falling feathers activate the founding rites
> and dances.
> The Way is open.

The journey together ends in the world of the spirit. Your relationship becomes a symbol that can activate fundamental energies in the world we live in. Because you understand what symbols can do, the Way will always be open to you. *Direction*: Re-imagine your situation. Gather energy for a decisive new move.

歸妹 ䷴ *54 Converting the Maiden* KUEI MEI

The marriage of the younger daughter; a passionate, irregular relationship; change over which you have no control; realize your hidden potential; desire, compulsion.

SETTING THE STAGE

Advancing will lead you to a place to marry. Thus there comes the time of Converting the Maiden. Accept this. Do not fear. Converting the Maiden leads to a woman's completion.

OPENING THE FIELD

Marry/convert, KUEI: give a young woman in marriage; transform, reveal hidden potential; return to where you belong; restore, revert; loyal. The ideogram shows a wife who has become mistress of a house.

Maiden, MEI: young girl who is not yet nubile; younger sister; daughter of a secondary wife; person in a servile position. The ideogram shows the graphs for woman.

THE RESPONSE

> Converting the Maiden.
> Chastising closes the Way and leaves no
> advantageous direction.

Converting the Maiden describes your relationship, or your part in it, in terms of a change you must go through which is beyond your control. The way to deal with it is to accept it and let yourself be led. The force involved is larger than you are. Though this relationship may be outside the rules, it could bring out who you really are. It proceeds in fits and starts and it moves forward through passion. You simply have to put up with it. If you try to impose order, or tell people what to do, the Way will close. The transformation needed here represents a deep, unacknowledged need. It is moving you to the place where you belong. Be adaptable and receptive. Move with the flow of events. The desire driving you is both an end and a new beginning. This is a very special situation that, though outside the norms, can lead to you to realize your hidden potential.

SYMBOL, REFLECTION AND PRACTICE

Thunder above Mists. Converting Maiden. Arousing energy stirs up your potential to stimulate and give things form. The solution is already underway.

Reflection: By facing and accepting the situation you are in, opportunities for new growth will come. Both of you have engineered this situation from deep inside you. What each is doing or has done, the other is doing or has done. You may find it in a different area of your lives. By facing the truth about yourselves, you will find it. Something is thrusting for release. You are both now finishing something and starting something new. Embrace the situation. Give yourselves time for acceptance and understanding to dawn. Open up to seeing your part in what is occurring.

Practice: Take time each day to contemplate the situation you are in. Bring each aspect of it into your awareness. As you do, affirm and keep affirming: "I accept" and "I am responsible". Dwell with the experiences stimulated by these affirmations. Ground yourself through your physical connection to the world around you.

Transforming Lines

INITIAL NINE
>Converting Maiden as a junior sister.
>A halting gait lets you tread.
>Chastising opens the Way.

You are not in a position of power, but that does not mean you can't influence things in your relationship and achieve your desire. Put yourself in order and do what you have to do. *Direction*: Release bound energy. The situation is already changing.

NINE AT SECOND
Squinting lets you observe things.
Divination: advantageous for people in the shadow.

Stay out of sight for now. Don't get involved in power struggles with your Friend. Look at things from an independent perspective. You will learn a lot this way, and be able to do whatever you want to do. *Direction*: A fertile shock is coming. Re-imagine the situation. Gather energy for a decisive new move.

SIX AT THIRD
Converting Maiden watches her hair growing.
You will reverse this marriage if you play
the junior sister.

Have patience, ease and courage with your Friend. In the end you will get everything you want. You will sabotage everything if you become a sycophant. *Direction*: Contain your great strength. Be resolute. You are connected to a creative force. Use it well.

NINE AT FOURTH
Converting Maiden overrunning the term.
Procrastinating in marrying lets you find
the right time.

Let things go in this relationship. Forget about deadlines and demands. This will increase your worth. Your Friend will appreciate it. You will know when it is the right time to act. *Direction*: A significant connection is approaching. Something important returns. Be open and provide what is needed.

Six at Fifth

> Supreme Burgeoning Converts the Maiden.
> Leading Wife's sleeves were not as fine as her
> Junior Sister's sleeves.
> The moon almost full. The Way opens.

An omen of great future happiness, fertility and power. Be like the moon that is almost full. Accept the secondary position willingly. It carries great power. Your love is assured. *Direction*: Express yourself. Find supportive friends. Gather energy for an important new move.

Six Above

> A woman carries a basket with no substance.
> A noble sacrifices a goat with no blood.
> There is no advantageous direction.

This relationship is an empty show: no substance, no blood, no passion. Nothing you can do will help. Don't make any more plans. Just leave. *Direction*: Turn conflict into creative tension. The situation is already changing.

豐 ䷶ *55 Abounding* FENG

**Plenty, copious, rich, generous, profusion; culminating
point, overflowing; activate inner creative energy;
sign of great change.**

SETTING THE STAGE

Acquiring a place through marriage means you will become
Great. Thus there comes the time of Abounding. Accept this.
Abounding means being Great. Abounding has many previous
causes.

OPENING THE FIELD

Abound, FENG: abundant harvest; fertile, plentiful, copious,
numerous; prolific, exuberant, overflowing; full, culminating,
ripe, sumptuous, luxurious; have many talents, friends, riches; too
much, exaggerated; eclipse, omen or sign of a great change. The
ideogram shows a horn of plenty.

THE RESPONSE

**Abounding will give you Success.
The King approaches the ancestral temple
to receive blessings for all.
Don't grieve!
The sun is really at the center of the sky.**

Abounding describes your relationship, or your part in it, in
terms of abundance and fertile profusion. The way to deal with it
is to be generous, open and joyous, connecting yourself to the
dark inner creative source. This is a time of prosperity and joy,
overflowing like the horn of plenty. Smile on each other and on
all your desires. Give with both hands. Don't let sadness enter
the picture. This will not last forever. Enjoy it deeply while it is

here. Be like the sun at midday, or the King who approaches the temple to receive blessing from the spirits and ancestors. Accept it all joyfully. No questions asked! Shed light on all. This is the fertile source of the coming harvest.

SYMBOL, REFLECTION AND PRACTICE

Thunder and lightning culminating. Abounding. Inner warmth and brightness permeate the world, rousing things to abundance. You can concentrate a great creative energy.

Reflection: Celebrate how well everything is going. Make the most of it. Give yourself ample time to enjoy the love and abundance you are now experiencing. Share it generously with others. During this high point, take thought for the way times change. Change is inevitable and trying to hang onto what you have will mean that you only lose it more quickly. Regularly pause to celebrate what you have, so that when the changes occur you are abundantly prepared. Spend time internally contemplating the completion of the harvest you can see ahead. Understand that your thoughts influence the outcome. Deliberately develop images of what is good for all. Imagine the outcome as an expression of your intention to support future growth and abundance.

Practice: Practice noticing how the richness of the present moment has been produced by past intentions. Cultivate optimistic, abundant, creative fantasies about the future. Notice the flow of life and avoid trying to hold onto what you have. This only leads to loss. Notice that cupped hands, when filled with water, immediately lose what they hold when you close your fists. Notice how the same thing happens with love, light, peace, laughter—with anything.

Transforming Lines

Initial Nine

> You meet your lord as an equal.
> Even if you stay a decade, it is not a mistake.
> Go on, you will be honored.

You meet someone who will change the course of your life. It is a deep mutual recognition. Stay with this person as long as you want to. It is not a mistake. If you hold onto the connection, it will bring you honor. *Direction*: A transition. Be very Small. Don't be afraid to act alone. You are connected to a creative force. Use it well.

Six at Second

> Abounding screens you.
> When the sun is at the center of the sky,
> You can see the Bin, constellation of fates.
> If you go forward now, you will only know
> doubts and affliction.
> Have confidence in a far-reaching
> connection to the spirit.
> The Way is open.

You can see things that other people can't see. Although you feel isolated from your Friend, don't act yet. Action will only bring you doubts and insults now. You have a profound connection to the spirits, which is working at a great distance to create connections. Fear not. The Way is opening. *Direction*: Rouse your sense of strength and purpose. Be resolute. You are connected to a creative force. Use it well.

Nine at Third

> Abounding profusion overwhelms you.
> When the sun is at the center of the sky,

You can see the froth of Small stars.
You break your right arm. This is not a mistake.

You are so overwhelmed and see such extraordinary sights that
you lose the capacity to act. Don't worry. This is not a mistake.
A new relationship is being born or an old one renewed.
Direction: A fertile shock is coming. Re-imagine your situation.
Gather energy for a decisive new move.

NINE AT FOURTH
Abounding screens you.
When the sun is at the center of the sky,
You can see the Bin, constellation of fates.
You meet your lord in hiding.
The Way is open.

You can see extraordinary things that most people can't begin to
understand. In this solitude and obscurity, you meet a Friend who
inspires and understands you. The recognition is immediate. Hold
onto the connection. The Way is open. *Direction*: Accept the difficult task. Release bound energy. The situation is already changing.

SIX AT FIFTH
Held in the beauty of the coming order.
There will be reward and praise.
The Way opens.

The next chapter in this relationship is full of beauty, joy and
love. Rewards and praise will be showered on you. The Way is
opening. *Direction*: Revolution and renewal. You are coupled
with a creative force. Use it well.

SIX ABOVE
Abounding roofs you in.
If you screen off your dwelling and peep through your door,

Living alone, without people.
For three years you will encounter no one.
The Way closes.

Your Friend may have hurt you, but now your melancholy and pain are in danger of isolating you. Break out of this trap! Don't shut yourself in. Grasp the changing time and act. If you don't, the Way will close. *Direction*: Become aware of your situation and join with others. Don't be afraid to act on your own. You are connected to a creative force. Use it well.

旅 ䷷ 56 *Sojourning* LÜ

Journeys, voyages, outside the social network; wander, exile; soldiers on a mission; quest, searcher, stranger in a strange land.

SETTING THE STAGE

When you exhaust the Great, you must let go of your residence. Thus there comes the time of Sojourning. Accept this. Do not fear. Sojourning means connecting the few.

OPENING THE FIELD

Sojourn/quest, LÜ: travel, journey, voyage; stay in places other than your home; visitor, lodger, temporary guest; outside the net of social beliefs, live in exile; search for your own way; a small group that has a common goal; soldiers on a mission; to be a stranger in a strange land. The ideogram shows people gathered around the symbol of a distant center.

THE RESPONSE

> **Sojourning, the Small will give you Success.**
> **Sojourning is an Advantageous Divination.**

Sojourning describes your relationship, or your part in it, in terms of wandering, temporary shelter, and an individual search. The way to deal with it is to realize your relationship or purpose comes from a distant center. You are outside the norm, traveling on a quest of your own. Stay Small and flexible. You can be successful here by adapting to each thing and not imposing your will. Together, consider things carefully. Make clear decisions even if they are painful. Limit your desires. This generates meaning and good fortune by releasing transformative energy. If you can do this, you will be able to connect with each other and find what you are seeking.

SYMBOL, REFLECTION AND PRACTICE

Fire above the Mountain. Sojourning. An inner limit gives you a real awareness of people and things. You can build up a great store of energy.

Reflection: You are on your own for now, even if you are with someone. The future may see you installed with people who are open and available to you, but you cannot count on this now. Think carefully about your goals with your Friend. Lower your expectations if they rely on good will and a receptive response from others. All the same, keep your primary attention on how you would like things to be. This will be a useful beacon as you travel through this time. Keeping private and to yourself can teach you much as you call on resources you don't currently know you have.

Practice: Have at least three conversations a day with people with whom you would like to be close. Be lightly friendly and undemanding emotionally. Notice how things evolve.

Transforming Lines

INITIAL SIX
Sojourning fragments, in fragments.
You split off from your place and grasp disaster.

This journey is falling apart before it has begun. You are grasping at petty details. Your Friend can't understand you. You are in imminent danger. Stop! Do you really want to act like this? *Direction*: Become aware of yourself! Don't be afraid to act on your own. You can be connected to a creative force. Use it well.

Six at Second

>   Sojourning, you approach a rest house.
>   Take care of your goods.
>   You acquire a young vassal.

You have found a way to come together, though you must still take care. You have also made a Friend who is willing to help you. *Direction*: You can establish something significant. Be resolute. You are connected to a creative force. Use it well.

Nine at Third

>   Sojourning, you burn down your rest house.
>   You lose your young vassal.
>   Divination: adversity.

You destroy what you have done through violent passions and you frighten your Friend away. Try to understand where this comes from. You are confronting danger that has its roots in the past. *Direction*: You will emerge and be recognized. Re-imagine the situation. Gather energy for a decisive new move.

Nine at Fourth

>   Sojourning, you find a place to abide.
>   You acquire goods and an emblem ax.
>   You say: "My heart is not glad."

You have found a place to be together, with responsibility and power to go with it. But these things bring sorrow, not happiness, for deep in your heart you know that you have forsaken what you really feel. *Direction*: Stabilize your desires. Release bound energy. The situation is already changing.

Six at Fifth

>   You shoot a pheasant. It disappears with one arrow.
>   Bringing this to completion brings you praise and a mandate.

You can complete your connection with one try. Your Friend will support you. Together, you can carry out your desires. This will bring you praise and much increased responsibility. *Direction*: Retire from an old involvement. You are coupled with a creative force. Use it well.

NINE ABOVE

> The bird burns down its nest.
> Sojourning people first laugh, then cry out and sob.
> You lose your cattle to change.
> The Way closes.

You are being careless and perhaps arrogant. You think you can take this relationship lightly, but you may soon have cause to lament. Everything you care about will vanish. You will soon be crying, not laughing. Consider your attitudes and change your heart or the Way will close to you. *Direction*: Be Small and be careful. Don't be afraid to act on your own. You are connected to a creative force. Use it well.

巽 ☴ 57 Gently Penetrating SUN

Gently penetrate to the heart; supple, flexible, subtle, determined; enter from below; support, nourish, the base or ground.

SETTING THE STAGE

You are sojourning and no place will simply accept you. Thus there comes the time of Gently Penetrating. Accept this. Do not fear. Gently Penetrating means entering the situation from below. Gently Penetrating means hiding your influence.

OPENING THE FIELD

Gently penetrate, SUN: enter into, put into, permeate, infiltrate; mild, subtle, docile; submit freely, be shaped by; penetrate to the core; support, foundation, base, nourish from below; wind, weather; wood, trees. The ideogram shows things on a base that supports and nourishes them.

Gentle Penetration is one of the Eight Helping Spirits. She works in those who lay out offerings. She penetrates to the heart. She is elegant and powerful, moving like wind and wood in the Earth. She is a healer, matches and couples the beings, lays out the offerings, brings each thing to its fate. She is a bright strutting cock, strong scented.

THE RESPONSE

Gently Penetrating, the Small will give you Success.
It is advantageous to have a direction to go.
It is advantageous to see the Great Person.

Gently Penetrating describes your relationship, or your part in it, in terms of the pervasive influence of the ground, wind and wood. The way to deal with it is to penetrate to this hidden ground through being supple and adaptable. Take the second place. Be accepting, supportive, flexible and subtle. Put the other's interests first and understand their situation deeply. Don't impose your will, but do have a clear direction. Talk to people who can help you and seek out the great in yourself. Be humble and hide your virtues. There is a powerful purpose moving here. Through subtle penetration you can connect with it and transform your relationship.

This is a pivoting phase, where change can occur quickly and fundamentally. If you want to alter your relationship, apply yourself now.

SYMBOL, REFLECTION AND PRACTICE
Following winds. Gentle Penetration connects the inner and outer worlds, beginning a new generation. You can turn discord into creative tension.

Reflection: The way forward is to create a gently, pervasive atmosphere that supports the outcomes you want. Doing many Small things creates this. Each day do something to enact the outcome you want: Say I love you, touch your Friend lightly and tenderly in passing, smile often and briefly, or stand your ground only very mildly. Do whatever you do unobtrusively, quietly and without intensity. Accepting that the process takes time, truly accepting this, adds great power to each act you take. Like many small drops of rain create the transforming power of a river, so your single acts will fill your relationship with the powerful flow of your intent.

Practice: Sit and imagine that a small replica of you is in your heart. Imagine that this figure is completely saturated with love. Encourage love energy to flood throughout your whole body and into the situation that surrounds you. Love performs miracles. Watch it work.

Transforming Lines

INITIAL SIX
**In advancing and withdrawing,
Act like a soldier for an Advantageous Divination.**

Make decisions with your Friend firmly and aggressively. Change directions as many times as you need to. Be decisive. If you hesitate you will undermine your real purpose. *Direction*: Accumulate the Small to achieve the Great. Turn conflict into creative tension. The situation is already changing.

NINE AT SECOND
**Penetrate gently beneath the bed.
Use historians and shamans in great number. The Way opens.
This is not a mistake.**

You must get to the core of this old story, full of sexual intrigue and dark ancestors. Use shamans, who can see the spirits, and historians, who know the past. Get to the bottom of it, see it in all its variety, and free your relationship from its grasp. This is not a mistake. *Direction*: Proceed step by step. Gather energy for a decisive new move.

NINE AT THIRD
Urgent penetrating, distress and confusion.

You are pushing your Friend too hard. This only produces confusion. You won't accomplish your desires like this. *Direction*: Dispel obstacles that stand in the way of understanding. Take things in. Be open and provide what is needed.

SIX AT FOURTH
> **The cause for sorrow disappears.**
> **In the fields you catch three kinds of game.**

You are finally in a position to act. You now have the information and recognition from your Friend that you need. You can achieve everything you desire. *Direction*: You are coupled with a creative force. Use it well.

NINE AT FIFTH
> **Divination: the Way is open. The cause for**
> **sorrow disappears.**
> **There is nothing that is not advantageous.**
> **If you initiate something now, it will not be completed.**
> **Before you take off the husk, three days.**
> **After you take off the husk, three days.**
> **The Way is open.**

Act now. Both of you will benefit. Don't start something new, but go through with what you have been planning. Watch it carefully before it is unveiled, and after it has begun. This is a very favorable time for the relationship. The Way is open. *Direction*: Renovate a corrupt situation. If you let yourself be led, you can realize hidden potential. The situation is already changing.

NINE ABOVE
> **Penetrating gently beneath the bed.**
> **You lose your goods and emblem ax.**
> **Divination: the Way closes.**

This is not the time to dig up the past. You will lose your possessions and your position. Leave it alone and be happy with what you have. If you start digging all over again, the Way will close. *Direction*: Connect with common needs and strengths. Turn conflict into creative tension.

兌 ䷹ 58 *Opening* TUI

Communication, self-expression; opportunity; pleasure, joy, excitement; persuade, exchange; the marketplace.

SETTING THE STAGE

When you enter something from below, you stimulate it. Thus there comes the time of Opening. Accept this. Do not fear. Opening means stimulation. Open means seeing and being seen.

OPENING THE FIELD

Open/expression, TUI: interact, interpenetrate, an open surface; opportunity; express yourself, persuade, cheer up, urge on; delight, pleasure, joy, excitement; responsive, free; gather, exchange, barter, trade; speech and words; the mists that rise from water. The ideogram shows a person speaking.

Open is one of the Eight Helping Spirits. She gladdens the heart. She speaks and spreads joy through the dancers and spirit-mediums. Open leads through joy and cheering words, magic and pleasure, song and dance. She feels the spirit in her body and gives it words. She is rising mists and open water. She gladdens all things that welcome her. She is a dancing goat and sheep.

THE RESPONSE

**Opening will give you Success
and an Advantageous Divination.**

Open describes your relationship, or your part in it, in terms of the opportunity for communication, pleasure and mutual exchange. The way to deal with it is to express yourself and your affection joyously and openly. Step outside of your normal views and situation. This is a time to connect with people and ideas you have never encountered before. Take great pleasure in things. Express yourselves openly. Cheer people on. Free yourselves from constraint. Let yourself be seen. Join together in talk and celebration. Exchange feelings and information. Yield to the power of joyous words and music. All this will bring your relationship to maturity.

This is a pivoting phase, where change can occur quickly and fundamentally. If you want to alter your relationship, apply yourself now.

SYMBOL, REFLECTION AND PRACTICE

Mists come together. Opening connects inside and out, stimulating and revealing the form of things. You can find the close relationship of people who dwell together.

Reflection: Talk to each other freely and often, both to keep communication open and to celebrate the joy in your connection with each other. Do the same with others, too. Keeping each other informed makes exciting and difficult times easier to manage, because everyone knows what is occurring. Open ongoing communication to achieve this. Speak directly and persuasively, avoiding any tendency towards harshness. Act with joy and kindness toward one another. This is a time for concentrating, too, on what you like about each other, encouraging each other on in what is important.

Practice: Each day, identify three things about yourself and your Friend that you like. Invite your Friend to do the same. Share with each other the six things you come up with. Celebrate together.

Transforming Lines

INITIAL NINE
Harmonious opening, the Way is open.

A beautiful connection. Expect real harmony to develop. The Way is open. Don't hold back. *Direction*: Look within to find the way out. Find supportive friends. Gather energy for a decisive new move.

Nine at Second

> **A connection to the spirits opens.**
> **The Way is open. The cause for sorrow disappears.**

This connection will open a whole new world. Reach out. The Way is open. Old sorrows and frustrations will simply vanish. *Direction*: Follow the stream of events. Proceed step by step. Gather energy for a decisive new move.

Six at Third

> **A coming opening. The Way closes.**

This may look like an interesting opportunity, but there is nothing in it. Turn away. The Way is closing. *Direction*: Be resolute. You are connected to a creative force. Use it well.

Nine at Fourth

> **Bargaining about this opening is not yet soothed.**
> **Limit the affliction and there will be rejoicing.**

You are discussing your connection and everyone's temperature is rising. Put a clear limit on negative emotions. If you actively bargain through seeking harmony, the situation will soon be filled with joy. *Direction*: Articulate your ideas. Take things in. Be open and provide what is needed.

Nine at Fifth

> **Connect to the spirits through stripping away**
> **the outmoded.**
> **There will be adversity.**

This opportunity for connection is dangerous and exciting. Though the relationship is filled with spirit, you must confront past memories and negative experiences. Strip away your old ideas and face up to the challenge. It is time to put the situation straight. *Direction*: If you let yourself be led, you can realize hidden potential. The situation is already changing.

Six Above

Extended opening.

Don't let go of this opportunity for connection. Draw it out as far as possible. Express yourself. Keep the possibilities open. You will be very sorry if you simply let go. *Direction*: Find supportive friends. Gather energy for an important new move.

渙 ䷸ 59 *Dispersing* HUAN

Dissolve, clear up, scatter; dispel illusions, break up obstacles, eliminate resistance; melt the rigid.

SETTING THE STAGE

You stimulate something, then it scatters abroad. Thus there comes the time of Dispersing. Accept this. Do not fear. Dispersing means that radiance and light dispel obstacles and create understanding.

OPENING THE FIELD

Disperse, HUAN: scatter clouds, clear away obstacles, dispel illusions, fear and suspicion; clear things up, dissolve resistance; untie, separate, change; mobilize the rigid, melt ice; fog lifting, mists clearing. The ideogram suggests changing form through expanding or scattering.

THE RESPONSE

Dispersing will give you Success.
The King approaches the Ancestral Temple
to receive blessings for all.
It is advantageous to step into the Great River.
This is an Advantageous Divination.

Dispersing describes your relationship, or your part in it, in terms of the possibility of clearing up obstacles, illusions and misunderstandings. The way to deal with it is to clear and dissolve what is blocking clarity and understanding. Break down the fears, illusions and suspicions that separate you. Eliminate confusion. Let the light of understanding shine through. Be like a King who approaches the temple to receive blessings for all from the spirits and ancestors. This is the right time to start a project or enterprise together. Step into the stream of life with a joint purpose.

Express yourself. Be clear and caring. Join hands and go on to achieve something great.

SYMBOL, REFLECTION AND PRACTICE

Wind moves above Stream. Dispersing. The inner stream penetrates and dissolves outer obstacles. You can nourish yourself and others now.

Reflection: Something that you share needs to dissolve. Good communication is needed, if you are to succeed. Get on with the process. Sort out where you are heading together and what your respective parts are. As communication difficulties arise, turn your attention to these and decide how to release yourselves from them. Make decisions together about what to do next on joint activities and follow through with action. Acting with confidence and a sincere heart.

Practice: Make time to dedicate what you do so you are living the Way. Do this individually or together. Start each day with this. Practice awareness in everything you do and demonstrate your commitment to living like this.

Transforming Lines

INITIAL SIX

> **Use the strength of a horse to rescue this.**
> **Invigorating opens the Way.**

Your relationship is in trouble, and you must come to the rescue. Give it all you've got. If you really rouse yourself, you can open the Way for the affection to flow. *Direction*: A deep and sincere connection. Take things in. Be open and provide what is needed.

NINE AT SECOND

> **Dispersing, fleeing your support.**
> **The cause for sorrow disappears.**

Let go of what you both habitually depend on. Open yourselves to the new. This will bring clarity and disperse the obstacles you are confronting. Your frustration will disappear and you will get what you desire. *Direction*: Let everything come into view. Strip away old ideas. Be open and provide what is needed.

SIX AT THIRD

> **Disperse your body.**
> **The cause for sorrow disappears.**

Don't identify with your need to express yourself or your craving for personal power. Focus entirely on the needs of your relationship now. That way there will be no cause for sorrow. *Direction*: If you let yourself be led, you can realize hidden potential. The situation is already changing.

SIX AT FOURTH

> **Disperse your flock. The Way to the Source is open.**
> **Disperse them and go to the hill-top shrine.**
> **You are not at all in hiding, this is a place to ponder.**

Let go of the flock of thoughts about your relationship that usually surround you. You have a great opportunity now, and you need to see it clearly. Go where you can talk to the spirits. This is not simply going into hiding. You need a place to ponder things deeply. The moment you do this, the new will come shining through. *Direction*: Stay out of quarrels and wrangles. Find supportive friends. Gather energy for an important new move.

NINE AT FIFTH

> **Dispersing sweat, a great outcry.**
> **Dispersing the King's residence.**
> **This is not a mistake.**

The two of you are involved in a great project. Don't think about anything else now. This is not a mistake. In the end this will correct your entire relationship. *Direction*: There is something immature in the situation that needs to be nourished. Take things in. Be open and provide what is needed.

NINE ABOVE

Disperse the bad blood.
Let it leave, send it away, then come forth.
This is not a mistake.

Remove any cause for conflict. Get rid of it. Send it far away. Then you can have the relationship you want and will make no mistakes. *Direction*: Take the risk. Take things in. Be open and provide what is needed.

節 ䷻ *60 Articulating* CHIEH

Sense the right time; measure, limit; articulate speech and thought; chapters, intervals, music and ceremonies; loyal and true.

SETTING THE STAGE

Things cannot simply radiate and disperse. Thus there comes the time of Articulating. Accept this. Do not fear. Articulating means stilling, finding the voice and the time.

OPENING THE FIELD

Articulate, CHIEH: Distinguish and join things; express ideas in speech; section, chapter, interval, unit of time; rhythm; months of the year, signs of the zodiac; limits, regulations, ceremonies, feasts, rituals; measure, economize, moderate, temper; firm, loyal, true; degrees, classes, levels. The ideogram shows the joints on a bamboo stalk.

THE RESPONSE

> **Articulating will give you Success.**
> **Divination: Bitter articulation will not allow putting your ideas to the trial.**

Articulating describes your relationship, or your part in it, in terms of finding the right relationship between things and the right times to act. The way to deal with it is make your connection articulate and graceful. Now is the time to define things in your lives. Create order and measure, ceremonies and feasts. Make things distinct and articulate how they go together. Create guides. Order your speech and your thoughts. Create a whole in which everything has a place, where everything can be celebrated. Do this in a spirit of love and warmth. Harsh rules and bitter speech cut you off from knowledge of each other and close the Way. By articulating things, you will keep your love from harm.

SYMBOL, REFLECTION AND PRACTICE

Stream above Mists. Articulating. Stimulating words from within articulate the stream of events. You can nourish yourself and others now.

Reflection: You need to prepare and organize. To get the most out of all your resources you need to know what they are and organize to use them well. Do this in a relaxed and accepting manner. You are looking for what will fit in, not trying to force things to fit. Getting together can help. Think of what each of you can do, what you are good at. Help each other, too. Then, while looking at the things you need to get done, use these qualities to decide how to do them. Press on with the job. It needs doing. Make sure, however, that you do it with grace and delicacy. Keep going and promote cooperation directly. Take initiative and responsibility.

Practice: Stay still for a short time each day. Imagine a small replica of you is sitting in the middle of your head. Allow energy to flood you there as you seek understanding of what you are doing and how you need to change things to do it. Only act when you know.

Transforming Lines

INITIAL NINE
Don't come out of the inner door and chamber.
This is not a mistake.

This is not a time to act. Stay in your place within the relationship. Contemplate what is important to you. This is not a mistake. *Direction*: You are facing a dangerous situation. Take things in. Be open and provide what is needed.

NINE AT SECOND
> **Not coming out of the outer gate and chamber,**
> **The Way closes.**

This is a time to act. Leave your habitual ways of thinking about your relationship. Enter the new. If you don't, you will surely regret it. The Way will close and you will be on the outside looking in. *Direction*: A new time is beginning. Give everything a place to grow. Strip away old ideas. Be open and provide what is needed.

SIX AT THIRD
> **If it is not like articulating, it will be like lamenting.**
> **This is not a mistake.**

You must set limits and create order in your relationship. If you don't, you will always be sorry. Everything will end in a flood of tears. If you articulate things now, you will make no mistake. *Direction*: Wait for the right moment to act. Turn conflict into creative tension. The situation is already changing.

SIX AT FOURTH
> **Quiet articulating. Success.**

Articulate your ideas and feelings quietly and peacefully to your Friend and you will meet a warm response. This creates success and inspires friends to join you. *Direction*: Express yourself and inspire others. Find supportive friends. Gather energy for a decisive new move.

NINE AT FIFTH
> **Sweet articulating opens the Way.**
> **Going on like this brings honor.**

Express yourself to your Friend with sweetness, grace and delight. The Way is open. You meet with honor and esteem. This is a significant time for you both. *Direction*: A significant connection is approaching. Something important returns. Be open and provide what is needed.

SIX ABOVE

Bitter articulating.
Divination: the Way closes.
The cause of sorrow disappears.

You are angry and frustrated. You want to impose harsh measures through bitter speech. Don't do it. You will do nothing but harm. If you will only give up your bitterness, the cause for sorrow will disappear. *Direction*: Connect your inner and outer lives. Take things in. Be open and provide what is needed.

中孚 ䷼ 61 Connecting to Center CHUNG FU

Sincere, truthful; connect your inner and outer lives; power of a heart at peace; connection to the spirit; a capture, spoils.

SETTING THE STAGE

You articulate something and then you make it trustworthy. Thus there comes the time of Connecting to Center. Accept this. Do not fear. Connecting to Center means being trustworthy.

OPENING THE FIELD

Connect, FU: accord between inner and outer; sincere, truthful, reliable, verified; have confidence; linked to and carried by the spirits; capture prisoners, take spoils; be successful. The ideogram shows a bird's claw holding a young animal, both protection and prey.

Center, CHUNG: inner, central, calm, stable; balanced, correct; put in the center, mediate, between; the inner life, the heart; a stable point that lets you face the vicissitudes of life. The ideogram shows an arrow fixed in the center of a target.

THE RESPONSE

Connecting to Center, little pigs and fishes.
It is advantageous to step into the Great River.
This is an Advantageous Divination.

Connecting to Center describes your relationship, or your part in it, in terms of a need to bring yourselves in accord with the truths of the heart. The way to deal with it is to make bringing your inner and outer lives together your central concern. Make what you want to do in the world coincide with what you know in your heart. Now is the time to be sincere, truthful and reliable. Empty your hearts of fear and greed. This brings pigs and fishes, fertility and abundance on all levels. Step into the stream of life together with a purpose. Let the expression of your inner connection permeate the world.

Symbol, Reflection and Practice

Wind above Mists. Connecting to Center. An open heart links the inner and outer worlds. You can nourish yourself and others.

Reflection: The spirit is close at hand. Bring it to fullness within you by balancing the inside and the outside, both individually and together. Your truth and the truth of others is the core of this. Expressing this and acting on it will create wonderful opportunities. Share openly with each other. Truth is a powerful means of uniting. Share what is most important to you. Notice the way your hearts are reflected in each other and in the events and people around you. Find how to bring all together, gently.

Practice: Each day, practice bringing your wisdom and love together. Imagine a small replica of you is in the middle of your head. Sitting in there, you are saturated with wisdom. Include awareness of the love in your heart from there. Alternatively, imagine a small replica of your Friend is in the middle of your heart. Sitting in there, you are saturated with love. Link with and include awareness of the wisdom in your head from there. Notice how the blending of the two changes things.

Transforming Lines

Initial Nine

Taking precautions now opens the Way.
If there are others involved, you will have no peace.

Stay alone and quiet and think about what you want to do. That will open the Way. If you are always worrying about your Friend, you will have no peace. Don't take on their problems now. *Direction*: Dispel illusions. Take things in. Be open and provide what is needed.

Nine at Second

> A calling crane in what is hidden.
> Its child is in harmony.
> It calls: "I have a beloved wine cup.
> Come to me and I will simply pour it out."

This is the profound call of one soul to another. Respond to it. It can change your life. Don't hesitate to answer your Friend. *Direction*: A flourishing time is coming. Increase your efforts. Strip away old ideas. Be open and provide what is needed.

Six at Third

> You acquire an antagonist.
> Perhaps you drum, perhaps you stop.
> Perhaps you weep, perhaps you sing.

Back and forth, again and again, there is very little you can do in this relationship. You have someone to love and fight with that you cannot defeat. This situation may trap you. In the end you will probably have to change it together or leave by yourself. *Direction*: Accumulate Small to achieve the Great. Turn conflict into creative tension. The situation is already changing.

Six at Fourth

> The moon is almost full.
> The horse's yoke disappears.
> This is not a mistake.

You are on your own now. A special moment. Your connections dissolve. Things are almost ripe. Don't be afraid to act alone. Preserve your integrity. This is not a mistake. It connects you with what is above. *Direction*: Make your way step by step. Turn conflict into creative tension. Gather energy for a decisive new move.

NINE AT FIFTH

> **This is a connection to the spirits**
> **that creates bonds between us.**
> **This is not a mistake.**

This relationship connects you on a deep spiritual level. This can truly help people. Put things right. Act energetically. This is not a mistake. *Direction*: Diminish your passions and involvement. Something significant is returning. Be open and provide what is needed.

NINE ABOVE

> **A soaring sound mounts to Heaven.**
> **Divination: the Way is closed.**

This is enthusiasm that flies above itself and carries you away. There is no real substance in this relationship. Ask yourself why you are doing this? The Way is closing. *Direction*: Set limits and articulate desires. Take things in. Be open and provide what is needed.

小過 ☷☶ *62 Small Traverses*
HSIAO KUO

A transition; adapt to each thing; be very careful, very Small; yin energy.

SETTING THE STAGE
When you trust something, it means you must move with it. Thus there comes the time of Small Exceeding. Accept this. Do not fear. Small Exceeding means moving beyond.

OPENING THE FIELD
Small, HSIAO: little, flexible, adaptable; humility, what is common to all; adapt to whatever happens; make things smaller, lessen, yin energy.
Traverse, KUO: go across, surpass, overtake; get clear of, get over; cross the threshold, surmount difficulties; transgress the norm, outside the limits.

THE RESPONSE
> Small Traverses will give you Success.
> This is an Advantageous Divination.
> It allows Small affairs,
> it does not allow Great affairs.
> The flying bird brings the sound as it leaves:
> "Above is not the proper place,
> below is the proper place."
> The Great Way is open.

Small Traverses describes your relationship, or your part in it, in terms of a transition through a great variety of different details and situations. The way to deal with it is to consider carefully and react to each thing in turn. If you are Small and careful, you can have your heart's desire. Adapt to each thing. Keep your powers hidden. Don't, under any circumstances, try to impose your will. This is not the time to try something big. Keep your sense of purpose. Listen to what the flying bird says: your place is below, not above. Don't go up, go down. This generates meaning and good fortune by releasing transformative energy. By being very careful and conscientious, the Great Way will open to you.

Symbol, Reflection and Practice
Thunder above mountain. Small Exceeding. An inner limit holds and confines outer expression. You can build up a great concentration of energy.

Reflection: Keep a low profile in what you do and take care of the details. This is a sensible thing to do and strengthening in the long run. Use restraint in all areas with each other. Even if others are trying to control things, avoid doing so yourself. Practice saying, "Yes" as your first response to others and to situations. Decide what to do from this accepting position, then act so as not to be seen.

Practice: Regularly spend time contemplating your inner experience of the situation you are in. Cultivate your complete availability to all the different inner experiences that emerge as you do. Let these wash through you and even take over your awareness, if they are strong enough. Once they have taken hold, sit with awareness of the seat beneath you. Do this until you reach equilibrium again. Notice how this releases you from acting impulsively.

Transforming Lines

Initial Six
Acting like a flying bird closes the Way.

Stay low, stay humble and stay grounded. Don't try to impress your Friend. Don't try to be the best. Don't fly away. If you do you will surely regret it. *Direction*: A time of abundance is coming. Continue on. You are connected to a creative force. Use it well.

SIX AT SECOND

> **Pass by your grandfather,**
> **meet your grandmother.**
> **Don't reach the Leader,**
> **meet his servant.**
> **This is not a mistake.**

Identify with people in secondary roles. Don't push yourself forward. Gladly accept the supporting position in your relationship. Don't try to dominate. You will see all your wishes fulfilled. The connections will have deep, enduring value. *Direction*: This has enduring value. Be resolute. It connects you to a creative force. Use it well.

NINE AT THIRD

> **You can do no more than defend yourself against this.**
> **If you carry on, you may be in grave danger.**
> **The Way closes.**

You are going beyond the safety limits here, moving into an impossible situation. If you are lucky, you can fend off harm. You are in real danger. Alone or together, you must stop acting like this. *Direction*: Gather resources so you can respond when the real call comes. Re-imagine the situation. Gather energy for a decisive new move.

NINE AT FOURTH

> **This is not a mistake.**
> **You nowhere pass it by, you meet it.**

> Let the adversity that is going now
> Be a necessary warning.
> Don't perpetually go back to the past.

The crisis is over and you have made the connection with your Friend. This is not a mistake. Take a look at the dangers your relationship has just passed through, the memories and ghosts. Let them be a warning. Don't go back! *Direction*: Stay humble and connected to the facts. Release bound energy. The situation is already changing.

SIX AT FIFTH

> Shrouding clouds, no rain.
> "They come from my western outskirts," you say.
> A prince with a string-arrow grasps another in a cave.

The culmination is coming. You make an enduring connection with someone who is in retreat. This relationship will open up a whole new life. *Direction*: A stimulating influence. It connects you with a creative force. Use it well.

SIX ABOVE

> You don't meet it, you pass it by.
> The flying birds scatter. The Way closes.
> This is called both a calamity and a blunder.

Danger and arrogance. Why are you being so stupid? You overreach yourself, flying higher and higher. This won't accomplish anything good for your relationship. A disaster from within and without. Change now! *Direction*: Step outside of the situation. Don't be afraid to act on your own. This will connect you to a creative force. Use it well.

63 *Already Fording*

既濟 ☲☵ CHI CHI

Begun, already underway, in progress; everything in place; proceed actively.

SETTING THE STAGE

When an excess of beings accumulate, it must bring about Fording the river of life. Thus there comes the time of Already Fording. Accept this. Do not fear. Already Fording means setting things right.

OPENING THE FIELD

Already, CHI: in progress, going on; completed, finished, mark of the past tense; thus, that being so. The ideogram shows a person eating, the meal already begun.

Ford, CHI: cross a river, overcome an obstacle, begin an action; bring help; succeed, bring to a conclusion. The ideogram shows water running in a ford.

THE RESPONSE

Already Fording. Success will come
through the Small.
This is an Advantageous Divination.
Initiating things opens the Way.
Bringing things to completion brings disorder.

Already Fording describes your relationship, or your part in it, in terms of an action that is already underway. The way to deal with it is to actively go on with what you are now doing and cooperate with the process. Adapt to what comes, don't try to impose your will. Everything is in place. This process can bring profit, insight and enjoyment to your relationship. It generates meaning and good fortune by releasing transformative energy. Continually refresh the situation. Keep coming up with new ideas. Put your energy at the service of the ongoing process of your love. Trying to push things to completion throws the relationship into disarray. Think about the problems and dangers you confront together. You are in exactly the right place. Carry on.

This is a pivoting phase, where change can occur quickly and fundamentally. If you want to alter your relationship, apply yourself now.

SYMBOL, REFLECTION AND PRACTICE

Stream above Fire. Already Fording. Inner awareness and the willingness to take risks create a stable situation. You can gather energy for an important new move.

Reflection: What you desire with your Friend has already started. Care is needed, however, so act with caution. Consider each other and the situation carefully. Do this together as much as you can. Combining your resources will bring the brightness of shared light to your understanding of what is necessary. Support each other in attempting modest gains related to immediate possibilities. Make a pact to alert each other, if either of you starts to try to do too much.

Practice: Spend time contemplating the completion of your future goal. Imagine that they are already completed. As you do, stay alert to your immediate physical environment. Do something, if a real opening emerges naturally.

Transforming Lines

Initial Nine

> **Pull your wheels back.**
> **Soak your tail.**
> **This is not a mistake.**

You have a great relationship, but you are starting too soon. Hold back. Start slowly. This is not a mistake. *Direction*: Re-imagine the situation. Gather your energy for a decisive new move.

Six at Second

> **A wife loses her veil.**
> **Don't pursue her.**
> **On the seventh day she will come.**

It seems like what you hope and care about in this relationship is lost. Don't worry. Don't chase it. When the time comes, it will find you without trying. Have no cares. You will have what you desire. *Direction*: Wait for the right moment to act. Turn conflict into creative tension. The situation is already changing.

Nine at Third

> **The High Ancestor subjugates souls on all sides.**
> **Three years go by and he controls them.**
> **Do not use Small people.**

The two of you are embarked on a great enterprise. It will take time to complete. Keep a firm purpose. Don't listen to what others try to tell you. Your hearts will win in the end. *Direction*: This is a new beginning. Strip away your old ideas. Be open and provide what is needed.

SIX AT FOURTH
> **Silk clothes in tatters, a token of what may come.**
> **Be careful until the day is through.**

Things look good, but they could change in a minute. Be careful.
The two of you are in the middle of an important passage. Don't
relax yet. Be vigilant. *Direction*: Revolution and renewal. This
couples you with a creative force. Use it well.

NINE AT FIFTH
> **The Eastern neighbor slaughters cattle.**
> **The offering of the Western neighbor**
> **was not like this.**
> **Live in the real and accept your blessing.**

Don't try to impress your Friend with an ostentatious display.
The sincerity of your feeling and your dedication to the relationship are what count most. Be yourself. Then accept the
blessing your sincerity brings. *Direction*: Accept the difficult task.
Release bound energy. The situation is already changing.

SIX ABOVE
> **Soaking your head.**
> **Adversity.**

You have gotten yourself in too deep. You are faced with dangers
you don't have the means to confront. Why go on like this?
Direction: Find supportive friends. Gather energy for a decisive
new move.

64 Not Yet Fording
WEI CHI

未
濟

On the edge of a change; gather your energy, everything is possible; wait for the right moment.

SETTING THE STAGE

Life cannot exhaust itself. Thus there comes the time of Not Yet Fording. Accept this fully and completely. Do not fear. Not Yet Fording means the masculine is exhausted and energy is gathering.

OPENING THE FIELD

Not Yet, WEI: has not yet occurred (but will occur in the course of time); incomplete, doesn't exist yet. The ideogram shows a tree that has not yet extended its branches.

Ford, CHI: cross a river, overcome an obstacle, begin an action; bring help; succeed, bring to a conclusion. The ideogram shows water running in a ford.

THE RESPONSE

> Not Yet Fording will give you Success.
> A Small fox arrives on a muddy bank.
> If she soaks her tail now,
> There will be no advantageous direction.

Not Yet Fording describes your relationship, or your part in it, in terms of being on the verge of an important change. The way to deal with it is to gather your energy and resources to make the crossing together. Hold back for now. Gather yourselves and make sure your plans are in order. You must make the crossing without getting stuck. Be like the small fox, a careful and clever animal who tries each step and can change direction quickly. Be prepared. If the fox crosses the ford to the mud of the other shore, then falls in and soaks her tail, all her work will be lost. So consider things carefully, but don't worry. There are forces gathering to move you into the right position.

> This is a pivoting phase, where change can occur quickly and fundamentally. If you want to alter your relationship, apply yourself now.

SYMBOL, REFLECTION AND PRACTICE

Fire above Stream. Not Yet Fording. An inner sense of risk holds radiance back in order to build up reserves of energy. You will soon be able to cross the stream of events.

Reflection: Wait for the right time. As you do, consider what you might do. Perhaps you have a joint goal already. Evaluate alternative ways of achieving it. Perhaps you do not have a goal. Look at the range of what you could do and think of the consequences. Support each other in the waiting process so you don't make mistakes by acting too early. The time will come.

Practice: Sit and remember previous times when your intent to act got ahead of the readiness of the situation. Remember the consequences of what you did. Apply what you learned then to this situation.

Transforming Lines

INITIAL SIX

> You soak your tail.
> Distress and confusion.

You start too soon and fall into the water. You don't understand yet this relationship, so hold back. *Direction*: Turn conflict into creative tension. The situation is already changing.

NINE AT SECOND

Pull your wheels back.
Divination: The Way opens.

Everything is loaded. You are ready to go. But don't start yet. By restraining your eager desires, you can truly open the Way. Think about what you want in this relationship. You are not quite ready yet. *Direction*: You will emerge and be recognized. Release bound energy. Gather energy for a decisive new move.

SIX AT THIRD

Not yet fording. Chastising closes the Way.
It is advantageous to step into the Great River.

On the edge of the great move. Don't try to discipline your Friend or set everything in order. Step into the river with a clear will and purpose. What you are beginning now will bring all you want. *Direction*: Ground yourself in the world of the spirit. Be resolute. You are connected to a creative force. Use it well.

NINE AT FOURTH

Divination: the Way is open.
The cause of sorrow disappears.
The power of Shake subjugates souls on all sides.
In three years there will be celebrations in the
Great City.

This is the time to act. The Way is open. Your misgivings about your Friend and this relationship will simply disappear. Arouse your energy. Get rid of the past. This may take a while, but in the end there will be great achievements. Your entire world will be transformed. *Direction*: You don't really understand the situation yet. Something significant is returning. Be open and provide what is needed.

SIX AT FIFTH

> **Divination: the Way is open.**
> **Without a cause for sorrow.**
> **This is the Relating Person's shining.**
> **There is a connection to the spirits.**
> **The Way is open.**

Act on your plans. The Way is open for this relationship. There is no sorrow in sight. Your sincere spirit will shine through. Sense what is important for you both. The spirits will help you. The Way is open. *Direction*: Stay out of quarrels and wrangles. Find supportive friends. Gather energy for a decisive new move.

NINE ABOVE

> **There is a connection to the spirit.**
> **Drink from the same cup. This is not a mistake.**
> **Immerse yourself. There is a connection to the spirits**
> **In letting go of what has passed.**

The voyage is over. Celebrate your accomplishments. The spirits will be there with the two of you. This is not a mistake. It is time to let go of the past. The joyous spirit will carry you forward. *Direction*: Release bound energy. The situation is already changing.

The Symbols of Love
by Name and Number

UPPER TRIGRAMS

LOWER TRIGRAMS		FORCE	FIELD	SHAKE	GORGE
	FORCE	1	11	34	5
	FIELD	12	2	16	8
	SHAKE	25	24	51	3
	GORGE	6	7	40	29
	BOUND	33	15	62	39
	PENETRATING	44	46	32	48
	RADIANCE	13	36	55	63
	OPEN	10	19	54	60

Key to the Symbols

UPPER TRIGRAMS

BOUND	PENETRATING	RADIANCE	OPEN	
26	9	14	43	FORCE
23	20	35	45	FIELD
27	42	21	17	SHAKE
4	59	64	47	GORGE
52	53	56	31	BOUND
18	57	50	28	PENETRATING
22	37	30	49	RADIANCE
41	61	38	58	OPEN

LOWER TRIGRAMS

Key to the Symbols